STUDY GUIDE

Alistair Younger
University of Ottawa

ABNORMAL PSYCHOLOGY
PERSPECTIVES
Third Edition

Philip Firestone
University of Ottawa

David J.A. Dozois
University of Western Ontario

PEARSON

Prentice
Hall

Toronto

ISBN 0-13-196744-4

Acquisitions Editor: Ky Pruesse
Developmental Editor: Patti Altridge
Production Editor: Charlotte Morrison-Reed
Production Coordinator: Janis Raisen

2 3 4 5   10 09 08 07

Printed and bound in Canada.

CONTENTS

PREFACE

Congratulations on purchasing the study guide to accompany **Abnormal Psychology: Perspectives** (3rd Edition). Your textbook is an excellent and up-to-date review of what is known about the major psychological disorders.

The study guide is designed to help maximize your learning of the material in the text. Each chapter begins with a **CHAPTER OUTLINE** that maps out the contents of the chapter in the text. I suggest you read through this outline before beginning your reading of the chapter, to get an idea of the major topics that will be covered. You may also use this outline to jot down any key terms and briefly note important points you come across in your reading. Next is a series of **LEARNING OBJECTIVES**. These take the form of brief, short-answer questions. After you have read the chapter, go through these objectives, and answer as many as you can. If you are unsure of an answer, this identifies an area that you should go back and re-read in the text. Next is the **KEY WORDS** section. Here we have listed all the key terms found in bold in the chapter. If you have a good understanding of the material you have read, you should be able to define each key word. If you are unsure about a term, you will find it listed with its page number on the last page of the chapter in the text. Go back and re-read the section where the term is found. The next section, **FILL-IN-THE-BLANKS**, allows you to test your knowledge of the material in the chapter by completing a series of fill-in-the-blank exercises. Go through and answer as many as you can. Then, check your answers against those at the end of the chapter in the study guide. Where you are unsure of an answer or where your answer was incorrect, go back and re-read that material in the text. The final section, **MULTIPLE CHOICE**, consists of a series of practice test questions drawn from the chapter. Upon completion of your study of the chapter, you should be able to answer each of these questions. To maximize your learning, try to be sure that you not only know which is the correct answer, but, also, why the alternative answers are incorrect. Answers to these questions are found at the end of the chapter in the study guide. As before, where you are unsure of an answer or are unsure as to why the alternatives are incorrect, re-read the relevant material in the text.

I prepared this study guide to be a valuable resource for you as you read and study your textbook. Using the study guide hand-in-hand with your text, completing all of the exercises as you complete your reading of each chapter in the text should be helpful in mastering the material in the text.

Good luck in your course!

CHAPTER 1

Concepts of Abnormality Throughout History

CHAPTER OUTLINE

LEARNING OBJECTIVES

When you have completed your study of the chapter, you should be able to:

1. Explain the key features of the following four attempts at defining abnormality: the statistical concept, personal distress, personal dysfunction, and violation of norms.

2. Identify and differentiate between four types of professionals involved in the mental health field.

3. Explain how the values of a particular society at a particular time are reflected in its view of the acceptability, treatment, and theories of the etiology of abnormal behaviour.

4. Explain what is meant by *trephination*. Discuss two alternative explanations for this practice.

5. Provide four examples of how Hippocrates explained psychological functioning in terms of bodily fluids or humours.

6. Describe how the ancient Arab world treated the mentally ill.

7. Discuss how mental illness was viewed in Europe in the Middle Ages. Describe the contributions to the more humane treatment of the mentally ill made by St. Teresa and St. Vincent de Paul.

8. Describe the typical conditions in the first asylums and workhouses.

9. Discuss the reforms made by Philippe Pinel in the treatment of the mentally ill.

10. Describe the contributions made by Emil Kraepelin to the diagnosis and classification of mental disorders.

11. Explain how the discovery of the link between syphilis infection and general paresis of the insane led to the prominence of somatogenesis as an explanation of mental disorders.

12. Describe the development of shock therapy as a treatment for mental disorders.

13. Describe the events that were significant in the development of psychopharmacological treatments for psychiatric disorders.

14. Discuss how hypnosis, psychoanalysis, and behaviourism contributed to the development of psychological approaches to mental disorders.

15. Trace the development of mental health services in Canada.

KEY WORDS

Psychological abnormality _____

_____

Mental illness _____

_____

Psychological disorder _____

_____

Psychopathology _____

_____

Culturally relative _____

_____

Psychiatrist _____

_____

Clinical psychologist _____

_____

Psychiatric nurse _____

_____

Psychiatric social worker _____

_____

Supernatural causes _____

_____

Natural causes _____

_____

Trephination _____

_____

Humours _____

_____

Asylums _____

_____

St. Vitus' Dance _____

_____

Bedlam _____

_____

Moral therapy _____

_____

Mental hygiene movement _____

_____

Syndromes _____

_____

General paresis of the insane (GPI) _____

_____

Somatogenesis_____

_____

Electroconvulsive therapy (ECT) _____

_____

Behaviourism _____

_____

Lobotomies _____

_____

FILL-IN-THE-BLANKS

1. The term *mental illness* is often used to convey the same meaning as psychological abnormality, but it implies a _____ rather than a psychological cause.

2. _____ refers to a prehistoric practice in which circular holes were cut in individuals' skulls, perhaps to release evil spirits.

3. Hippocrates claimed that hysteria was the result of a wandering _____.

4. Plato suggested that dreams served to satisfy desires because the inhibiting influences of the higher faculties were not present during sleep. This view foreshadowed _____'s theory of dreams.

5. According to Martin Luther, if the devil possessed people corporally, they would become _____, but if he possessed them spiritually, they should be considered _____.

6. As the association between mental illness and possession by the devil became more popular during the Middle Ages, _____ was frequently used to treat individuals thought to be possessed.

7. During the period of the Spanish Inquisition, _____ defended the mentally ill by claiming they were sick.

8. Appointed director of La Bicêtre in 1792, _____ ordered dramatic reforms in the treatment of the inmates.

9. Kraepelin attempted to classify mental disorders into groups of co-occurring symptoms that he referred to as _____.

10. Krafft-Ebing demonstrated that general paresis was a long-term consequence of _____ infection.

11. The term _____ refers to the notion that psychopathology is caused by biological factors.

12. Electroconvulsive therapy was initially used only with _____. It was later found to be most effective with patients suffering from _____, with whom it is still used to this day.

13. Josef Breuer employed _____ with hysteria patients in order to have them talk freely about, and relive, unpleasant past events that he believed caused their disorder. Breuer called this treatment the _____ method.

14. Surgical removal or disconnection of the frontal lobes of the brain, referred to as _____, was widely used in Canada from the mid-1940s until the mid-to-late 1960s.

MULTIPLE CHOICE

1. Which of the following is true concerning abnormality?

   a. Abnormal behaviour tends to occur infrequently in the population.
   b. All infrequent behaviour should be considered abnormal.
   c. All abnormal behaviour occurs infrequently.
   d. All of the above.

2. Hippocrates proposed that listlessness resulted from an overabundance of

   a. black bile   b. phlegm
   c. yellow bile   d. blood

3. Methodism regarded mental illness

   a. as resulting from supernatural causes beyond the understanding of ordinary mortals
   b. as resulting from disturbances in bodily fluids or humours
   c. as resulting from either a constriction of body tissue or as a relaxation of those tissues due to exhaustion
   d. as the consequence of possession by the devil or his minions.

4. In the Middle Ages, Martin Luther made a distinction between

   a. mind and body   b. supernatural and natural causes
   c. sanity and insanity   d. madness and witchcraft

5. During the waning years of the Middle Ages, there arose in Europe an epidemic of mass hysteria, known as _____, where groups of people would be seized by an irresistible urge to leap about, jumping and dancing, and sometime convulsing.

   a. general paresis of the insane   b. bedlam
   c. trephination   d. St. Vitus' Dance

6. During the period of the Spanish Inquisition, St. Teresa of Avila defended the mentally ill by

   a. treating them with an early form of hypnotism
   b. claiming they were sick
   c. raising funds by charging the public a fee to visit the institution
   d. allowing mentally ill individuals to live with local families

7. St. Vincent de Paul

   a. declared that it was the responsibility of society to develop means to relieve mentally ill people of their suffering
   b. established workhouses for the poor, the old, and the insane
   c. developed a systematic and statistically based approach to the classification, management, and treatment of disorders
   d. was the first to view mental disorders as disruptions in nervous system functioning

8. Phrenology was the field of study that argued that

   a. deviations from normal functioning are transmitted by hereditary processes and that these deviations progressively degenerate over generations
   b. all mental disorders are the result of biological problems
   c. mental disorders are the result of an infection of some sort
   d. criminality is inherited and can be identified by the shape of a person's skull

9. The first individual to recognize that different disorders not only had distinct features but also differed in terms of the age of onset of the disorder and their typical course over time was

   a. Mesmer
   c. Kraepelin
   b. Watson
   d. Krafft-Ebing

10. Shock therapy initially involved treatment with

    a. electric shock
    c. curare
    b. insulin
    d. acetylcholine

11. Electroconvulsive therapy has been found to be most effective with patients suffering from

    a. schizophrenia
    c. major depression
    b. anxiety disorders
    d. seizures

12. The first neurotransmitter was isolated in 1926, by Otto Loewi, who identified the action of _____ as mediating nerve impulses within the brain.

    a. acetylcholine   b. chlorpromazine
    c. phenothiazine   d. antihistamine

13. Anton Mesmer argued that hysteria resulted from

    a. a misaligned uterus
    b. forgotten unpleasant events from the past
    c. a disturbed distribution of magnetic fluid
    d. a break in the organized system of thought and emotion

14. Joseph Breuer employed _____ in the treatment of patients suffering from hysteria.

    a. harsh discipline and frequent beatings
    b. insulin shock
    c. antihistamines of the phenothiazine group of drugs
    d. hypnosis

15. According to John B. Watson, abnormal behaviour was the result of

    a. unfortunate conditioning experiences
    b. a break in the organized system of thought and emotion
    c. unpleasant past events that the patient had forgotten
    d. the effects of labelling a person as abnormal

16. The first asylum for the mentally ill in Canada was located in

    a. Halifax   b. Toronto
    c. Quebec   d. Charlottetown

17. Dr. Ewen Cameron is probably best known for

    a. his pioneering research into lobotomies
    b. his role in identifying the importance of neurotransmitters
    c. his theorizing concerning the importance of conditioning in the development of abnormal behaviour
    d. his brainwashing experiments during the late 1950s and early 1960s

18. Dr. Ruth Kajander was one of the first psychiatrists in North America to

    a. employ cognitive-behavioural therapy as treatment for psychological disorders
    b. study how aggressive behaviour was acquired in childhood
    c. recognize the potential of a major tranquilizer in the treatment of schizophrenia
    d. recognize the value of ECT as a treatment for depression

ANSWERS

FILL-IN-THE-BLANKS

1. medical
2. trephination
3. uterus
4. Freud
5. mad; witches
6. exorcism
7. St. Teresa
8. Philippe Pinel
9. syndromes
10. syphilis
11. somatogenesis
12. schizophrenia; major depression
13. hypnosis; cathartic
14. lobotomy

MULTIPLE CHOICE

1.	a	10.	b
2.	b	11.	c
3.	c	12.	a
4.	d	13.	c
5.	d	14.	d
6.	b	15.	a
7.	a	16.	c
8.	d	17.	d
9.	c	18.	c

CHAPTER 2

Theoretical Perspectives on Abnormal Behaviour

CHAPTER OUTLINE

The Biopsychosocial Model

LEARNING OBJECTIVES

When you have completed your study of the chapter, you should be able to:

1. Contrast single-factor and interactionist explanations.

2. Describe three essential features of scientific theories.

3. Explain the general aims of theories about mental disorders.

4. Describe three ways in which biological theories explain mental disorder.

5. Identify the primary functions of the hindbrain, midbrain, and forebrain.

6. Describe how neurotransmitters carry messages from one neuron to the next.

7. Discuss four ways in which disturbances in neurotransmitter systems can result in abnormal behaviour.

8. Describe the functions of the somatic nervous system and the two systems making up the autonomic nervous system (sympathetic and parasympathetic nervous systems).

9. Explain how the endocrine system interacts with the central nervous system.

10. Explain how researchers investigate the genetic bases of psychiatric disorders.

11. Identify and describe the three levels of consciousness proposed by Freud.

12. Describe the major functions of each of the following structures of personality: id, ego, and superego.

13. Outline Freud's five stages of psychosexual development, describing the major features of each stage.

14. Explain the role of defence mechanisms in Freud's theory. Identify eight defence mechanisms described by Freud, providing examples for each.

15. Describe how Watson and Rayner classically conditioned fear in little Albert.

16. Discuss how Mowrer integrated principles of both classical and operant conditioning into a two-factor explanation of the acquisition and maintenance of phobias.

17. Describe the differences between positive and negative reinforcement, and between positive and negative punishment.

18. Discuss how social learning theory, particularly cognitive-behavioural theory, differs from classical and operant conditioning.

19. Explain how irrational beliefs and cognitive schemata may underlie psychological disorders, according to Ellis and Beck.

20. Describe the basic concepts of Rogers's person-centred theory.

21. Outline Maslow's hierarchy of needs.

22. Identify the major assumptions of the existential approach.

23. Define what is meant by *labelling theory,* and describe the results of Rosenhan's research into the effects of psychiatric labelling.

24. Discuss how social support, gender, and race and poverty can be influential in mental disorders.

25. Describe the major assumptions of systems theory.

26. Explain the diathesis-stress perspective, providing examples of biological and psychological diatheses and stressors.

27. Explain what is meant by the term *biopsychosocial model*.

KEY WORDS

Single-factor explanations _____

_____

Interactionist explanations _____

_____

Null hypothesis _____

_____

Etiology _____

_____

Dementia _____

_____

Neurotransmitters _____

_____

Brain plasticity _____

_____

Behavioural genetics _____

_____

Genotype-environment interaction _____

_____

Concordance _____

_____

Genetic linkage studies _____

_____

Molecular biology _____

_____

Psychodynamic _____

_____

Conscious _____

_____

Preconscious _____

_____

Unconscious _____

_____

Id _____

_____

Ego _____

_____

Superego _____

_____

Libido _____

_____

Phallic stage _____

_____

Oedipal complex _____

_____

Electra complex _____

_____

Defence mechanisms _____

_____

Classical conditioning _____

_____

Operant conditioning _____

_____

Reinforcement _____

_____

Punishment _____

_____

Social learning theory _____

_____

Cognitive-behavioural theory _____

_____

Self-efficacy _____

_____

Rational-emotive behaviour therapy _____

_____

Content specificity _____

_____

Self-actualization _____

_____

Labelling theory _____

_____

Systems theory _____

_____

Diathesis-stress perspective _____

_____

Biopsychosocial model _____

_____

FILL-IN-THE-BLANKS

1. Theories gain in strength, not just because the evidence supports their positions but primarily because alternative explanations are _____.

2. It is perhaps better to think of brain activity related to particular functions or actions not as *located* in a single area of the brain but as _____ in one or more areas.

3. The hindbrain primarily directs the functioning of the _____ nervous system, which in turn controls primarily internal activities, such as digestion, cardiovascular functioning, and breathing.

4. _____ are the chemical substances that carry the messages from one neuron to the next in the complex pathways of nervous activity within the brain.

5. The autonomic nervous system (ANS) has two parts: the _____ nervous system and the _____ nervous system.

6. Freud and Breuer viewed _____, that is discharging emotional responses attached to unconscious memories, as the effective element in treating many problems.

7. For Freud, the _____ was the most important level of the mind. All our biological drives, particularly sexual and aggressive drives, reside at this level.

8. The ego _____ *(is/is not)* concerned with what is right or wrong, as it functions to curb the desires of the id.

9. The expression of libidinal energy is focused on different body parts, called _____ zones, that differ at different stages of development, according to Freud.

10. During the phallic stage, boys are presumed to develop sexual desires for their mother and view their father as a competitor, which Freud described as the _____ complex.

11. The defence mechanism of _____ involves hiding the real issues behind a screen of abstract analyses.

12. Although people with phobias repeatedly encounter their phobic stimulus without any dreadful consequences occurring, their phobias nevertheless persist. To explain this fact, Mowrer developed what came to be known as the _____ theory of conditioning.

13. According to Bandura (1989), _____ concerns the set of beliefs people have "about their capabilities to exercise control over events that affect their lives."

14. According to Ellis's rational-emotive therapy, _____ beliefs distort responses, making the person's behaviour dysfunctional.

15. According to Beck's approach, people with disorders have underlying cognitive _____ that inappropriately direct their processing of information, resulting in distortions of attention, memory, and comprehension.

16. Rollo May and Viktor Frankl are the leading proponents of the _____ view, as applied to human problem behaviour. Both these theorists see the struggle to find _____ in our lives and our acceptance of responsibility for our choices as critical in understanding human behaviour.

17. _____ theory proposes that the whole is more than the sum of its parts.

18. According to the _____ perspective, a predisposition to develop a disorder, interacting with the experience of stress, causes mental disorders.

MULTIPLE CHOICE

1. Thought, speech, perception, memory, learning, and planning are controlled by the

   a. hindbrain
   b. forebrain
   c. midbrain
   d. reticular activating system

2. Pleasure-seeking and exploratory behaviours seem to be associated with the neurotransmitter _____.

   a. dopamine
   b. serotonin
   c. norepinephrine
   d. gamma aminobutyric acid

3. The neurotransmitter _____ seems to be associated with the constraint or inhibition of behaviour.

   a. serotonin   b. dopamine
   c. epinephrine   d. norepinephrine

4. Which of the following disorders is not related to malfunctioning endocrine glands?

   a. dementia
   b. cretinism
   c. hypoglycemia
   d. Actually, all of the above *are* related to endocrine malfunction.

5. Patients suffering from generalized anxiety disorder are described as _____ because they consistently show less responsivity on ANS measures of arousal.

   a. underarousable
   b. affectively flat
   c. hyporesponders
   d. autonomic restrictors

6. In genetic linkage studies, researchers examine families that have a high incidence of a particular psychiatric disorder. They look for the presence of particular traits, called _____, that can be linked to the occurrence of the disorder.

   a. concordant traits
   b. biological indicators
   c. genetic markers
   d. inherited dispositions

7. The _____ holds information not presently within our awareness but that can readily be brought into awareness.

    a. conscious
    b. preconscious
    c. unconscious
    d. subconscious

8. As the individual learns which expressions of desires are practical and possible, the ego comes to be governed by the

    a. moral principle
    b. pleasure principle
    c. conscious principle
    d. reality principle

9. The _____ is the personality structure that, according to Freud, is present at birth and contains the biological or instinctual drives.

    a. ego
    b. superego
    c. id
    d. alterego

10. In Freud's view, failure to resolve a psychosexual stage would result in a _____ the erogenous zone associated with that stage.

    a. fixation on
    b. repression of
    c. oppression of
    d. suppression of

11. During the _____ stage, girls experience what Freud referred to as the Electra complex.

    a. anal stage
    b. phallic stage
    c. latency stage
    d. oral stage

12. Artists who paint nudes may be displaying the Freudian defence mechanism of

    a. displacement
    b. projection
    c. denial
    d. sublimation

13. Watson and Rayner conditioned fear in Little Albert by pairing a white rat with a sudden loud noise. In this study, the loud noise served as the

    a. UCR
    b. CS
    c. CR
    d. UCS

14. A teenager's father tells him that because he stayed out past curfew last week, his use of the family car is cut off for one week. This is an example of

    a. negative punishment
    b. positive reinforcement
    c. negative reinforcement
    d. positive punishment

15. Phobias persist in spite of people encountering their phobic stimulus without any dreadful consequences occurring. According to two-factor theory, this is because

    a. people learn to escape and avoid the phobic stimulus, which is positively reinforced by an increase in anxiety
    b. people learn to escape and avoid the phobic stimulus, which is negatively reinforced by a reduction in anxiety
    c. people learn to escape and avoid the phobic stimulus, which is positively punished by an increase in anxiety
    d. people learn to escape and avoid the phobic stimulus, which is classically conditioned by a reduction in anxiety

16. Both Ellis and Beck see the job of the cognitive therapist as

    a. helping clients to accept themselves and to rely on themselves for personal evaluations
    b. helping clients to realize their personal potential
    c. helping clients to recognize and correct distorted beliefs
    d. helping clients take personal responsibility for their own actions and those of significant others in their lives

17. According to Maslow's approach, once physiological needs, along with safety needs, have been met, the individual then can meet the next set of needs in the hierarchy, which are

    a. self-actualization needs
    b. self-worth needs
    c. belongingness needs
    d. existential needs

18. When Rosenhan had eight pseudo-patients admitted to a psychiatric hospital under the erroneous diagnosis of schizophrenia

    a. the hospital staff immediately recognized that these people were not really schizophrenic and released them
    b. the pseudo-patients had great difficulty convincing the staff that they were schizophrenic
    c. the labelling of the pseudo-patients as disordered caused the hospital staff to interpret their normal behaviour as abnormal
    d. the pseudo-patients themselves began to question their own sanity after being diagnosed as schizophrenic

ANSWERS

FILL-IN-THE-BLANKS

1. rejected
2. concentrated
3. autonomic
4. neurotransmitters
5. sympathetic; parasympathetic
6. catharsis
7. unconscious
8. is not
9. erogenous
10. Oedipal
11. intellectualization
12. two-factor
13. self-efficacy
14. irrational
15. schemas
16. existential; meaning
17. systems
18. diathesis-stress

MULTIPLE CHOICE

1.	b	10.	a
2.	a	11.	b
3.	a	12.	d
4.	a	13.	d
5.	d	14.	a
6.	c	15.	b
7.	b	16.	c
8.	d	17.	c
9.	c	18.	c

CHAPTER 3

Classification and Diagnosis

CHAPTER OUTLINE

The Perfect Diagnostic System

The History of Classification

DSM-IV-TR: A Multiaxial Approach

Categories of Disorder in DSM-IV-TR

Disorders Usually First Diagnosed in Infancy, Childhood, or Adolescence

Delirium, Dementia, Amnesia, and Other Cognitive Disorders

Substance-Related Disorders

Schizophrenia and Other Psychotic Disorders

Mood Disorders

Anxiety Disorders

Somatoform Disorders

Factitious Disorders

Dissociative Disorders

Sexual and Gender Identity Disorders

Eating Disorders

Sleep Disorders

Impulse Control Disorders

Adjustment Disorders

Personality Disorders

Other Condition that May Be a Focus of Clinical Attention

ISSUES IN THE DIAGNOSIS AND CLASSIFICATION OF ABNORMAL BEHAVIOUR

Against Classification

Criticisms Specific to DSM

The Prevalence of Mental Disorders

LEARNING OBJECTIVES

When you have completed your study of the chapter, you should be able to:

1. Explain the differences between an assessment and a diagnosis.

2. Understand how a perfect diagnostic system would function, as well as know the limitations that such a system currently faces in practice.

3. Identify and describe the six functions of a good classification system.

4. Outline the various milestones in the history of classification, from Kraepelin's early efforts to the completion of the DSM-IV-TR.

5. Describe the five axes comprising DSM-IV-TR's multiaxial classification system. Explain the major advantage of a multiaxial classification system to diagnosis.

6. Identify and briefly describe the categories of disorders listed in Axis I and Axis II of the DSM-IV-TR.

7. Identify and discuss three main arguments against classification.

8. Contrast the categorical and dimensional approaches to classification, describing the advantages and disadvantages of each. Give an example of a disorder that would fit well under each approach.

9. Describe the two necessary qualities that any measurement tool must have.

10. Define *inter-rater reliability* and identify the factor that is most responsible when it is low.

11. Identify and describe the two most important types of validity for diagnostic systems.

12. Explain how gender bias can influence a diagnosis.

13. Explain how cultural factors may influence the diagnostic process.

14. Outline some of the current thinking toward classification and diagnosis.

15. Discuss the following: Are mental disorders overdiagnosed?

KEY WORDS

Diagnosis _____

_____

Diagnostic system_____

_____

Assessment _____

_____

Polythetic _____

_____

Major depressive disorder _____

_____

Mania _____

_____

Bipolar conditions_____

_____

Comorbidity _____

_____

Categorical _____

_____

Dimensional _____

_____

Reliable _____

_____

Valid _____

_____

Inter-rater reliability _____

_____

Concurrent validity _____

_____

Predictive validity _____

_____

FILL-IN-THE-BLANKS

1. A diagnosis is made on the basis of a _____: a system of rules for recognizing and grouping various types of abnormalities.

2. The *Diagnostic and Statistical Manual* (DSM) was published by the _____ in 1952.

3. One of the major innovations of DSM-III was the use of a _____ approach to classification.

4. Axis III from DSM-IV-TR covers any _____ disorder that might be relevant to the understanding or management of a particular case.

5. In bipolar conditions, both _____ and _____ are exhibited.

6. In _____ disorder, the person reports the loss of motor or sensory function—for example, a paralysis or blindness.

7. Individuals with _____ disorder have an apparent psychological need to assume the role of a sick person.

8. In _____ disorders there is a sudden and profound alteration in consciousness that affects an individual's memory and identity.

9. As many as 50 percent of people suffering from anxiety disorders also have mood disorders. This is an example of _____.

10. A substantial number of professionals argue that the whole diagnostic endeavour is flawed because of its adherence to the _____ model.

11. Jerry, who is a skilled musician with a strong social conscience and a volatile temper, has been diagnosed with schizophrenia. Once diagnosed, he is seen simply as a "schizophrenic." This is an example of _____.

12. The _____ approach to classification measures disorders on a continuum, ranging from nonexistent or mild to severe, whereas the _____ approach is concerned with whether or not an individual has a disorder, with no in-between.

13. The usefulness of any measurement tool rests on two qualities: it must be _____ and _____.

14. In a classic study on the reliability of the diagnostic process (Beck et al., 1962), it was determined that the inadequacy of the DSM-I diagnostic system itself was by far the factor most responsible for poor _____ reliability.

15. Some writers have claimed the DSM describes many psychiatric disorders in a fashion that makes a diagnosis more probable for _____ (men/women), even when no pathology is involved.

16. DSM-IV-TR strives to be atheoretical and to take _____ differences into account.

17. DSM-IV-TR stresses _____ behaviour and provides _____ rules for diagnosis.

MULTIPLE CHOICE

1. Which of the following is untrue?

   a. A diagnosis consists of a determination or identification of the nature of a person's disease or condition.
   b. An assessment is a procedure in which information is gathered systematically in the evaluation of condition.
   c. A psychiatric assessment may include the completion of self-report scales or other report rating scales.
   d. Information from each of the diagnostic procedures contributes to the formulation of an assessment.

2. DSM-III-R was developed to be _____, meaning that an individual could be diagnosed with a certain subset of symptoms, without having to meet all criteria.

   a. multimodal
   c. nomothetic
   b. multilinear
   d. polythetic

3. A milestone in the modern development of a comprehensive diagnostic scheme was the decision by _____ to add mental health disorders to the International List of the Causes of Death.

    a. the *Diagnostic and Statistical Manual* (DSM)
    b. the World Health Organization (WHO)
    c. the American Psychiatric Association (APA)
    d. Kraepelin

4. In 1980 the APA published

    a. DSM
    b. DSM-II
    c. DSM-III
    d. DSM-III-R

5. Bill has problems with his primary social support group. Under which axis of the DSM-IV-TR multiaxial classification system would his difficulties fall?

    a. Axis II
    b. Axis III
    c. Axis IV
    d. Axis V

6. Axis V, the Global Assessment of Functioning Scale (GAF Scale) of DSM-IV-TR, scored on a maximum of

    a. 10
    b. 50
    c. 100
    d. 500

7. An _____ is a recurrent, unwanted, and intrusive thought.

    a. obsession
    b. compulsion
    c. phobia
    d. paraphilia

8. Comorbidity

   a. although common, is rarely present more than half the time
   b. means that it is possible for an individual to meet the diagnostic criteria for more than one diagnostic condition
   c. clearly outlines the nature of the relationship between anxiety and mood disorders
   d. all of the above

9. _____ is a dissociative disorder.

   a. Somatization disorder
   b. Conversion disorder
   c. Depersonalization disorder
   d. Body dysmorphic disorder

10. Sleep terror disorder and sleepwalking disorder are examples of

    a. dyssomnias
    b. parasomnias
    c. a dyssomnia and a parasomnia, respectively
    d. other conditions that may be a focus of clinical attention

11. Stigmatization is mostly the result of

    a. flaws in the diagnostic system
    b. people's reactions
    c. the accuracy of the diagnosis itself
    d. the school of thought held by the clinician making the diagnosis

12. Which is not a disadvantage of a categorical approach?

    a. It does not recognize the continuum between normal and abnormal.
    b. Some people may be denied help because they fall just short of the diagnostic criteria.
    c. It does not give a meaningful description of an individual's psychological problems.
    d. Increased diagnoses could burden the mental health system.

13. The two most important types of validity for diagnostic systems are

    a. construct and predictive
    b. concurrent and predictive
    c. construct and criterion
    d. criterion and predictive

14. In a diagnostic system

    a. validity and reliability are completely independent from each other
    b. there is a system of rules for recognizing and grouping various types of abnormalities
    c. reliability depends inexorably on validity
    d. reliability is determined by whether a diagnostic category is able to predict behavioural and psychiatric disorders accurately

15. Which of the following is true concerning the DSM and gender bias?

    a. Some stereotypic feminine behaviours may be seen as signs of emotional immaturity and psychopathology.
    b. In the late 1960s, there were few if any criticisms of gender bias and sexism in the mental health system.
    c. DSM-I and DSM-II tried hard to steer clear of psychoanalytic theory, which had been extensively charged with sexism.
    d. DSM-III achieved complete freedom from gender bias.

16. DSM-IV-TR

    a. has been criticized for the way that all five axes seem to correspond to exaggerated female stereotypes
    b. has been criticized for using categories that do not do justice to the complexity of human behaviour
    c. has striven toward being theoretical and has neglected to take cultural differences into account
    d. has avoided many of the cultural and professional assumptions that have characterized previous DSM editions

17. A high score on the F subscale of the MMPI

    a. may indicate an inability to understand the questions
    b. may reflect a different cultural background in the responder
    c. may indicate careless answering on the part of the responder
    d. all of the above

18. The Ontario Health Survey

    a. is one of the most comprehensive and well-constructed epidemiological studies to date
    b. produced results that were quite different from those reported in other provinces
    c. interviewed between 800 and 1000 people
    d. has been criticized because it interviewed only people living in institutions

ANSWERS

FILL-IN-THE-BLANKS

1. diagnostic system
2. American Psychiatric Association
3. multiaxial
4. medical
5. depression, mania
6. conversion
7. factitious
8. dissociative
9. comorbidity
10. medical
11. stigmatization (or labelling)
12. dimensional; categorical
13. reliable; valid
14. inter-rater
15. women
16. cultural
17. observable; explicit

MULTIPLE CHOICE

1.	d	10.	b
2.	d	11.	b
3.	b	12.	d
4.	c	13.	b
5.	c	14.	b
6.	c	15.	a
7.	a	16.	b
8.	b	17.	d
9.	c	18.	a

CHAPTER 4

Psychological Assessment and Research Methods

CHAPTER OUTLINE

ASSESSMENT

Assessment Tools: Striving for the Whole Picture

Reliability and Validity

Clinical vs. Actuarial Prediction

BIOLOGICAL ASSESSMENT

Brain Imaging Techniques

Neuropsychological Testing

PSYCHOLOGICAL ASSESSMENT

Clinical Interviews

Assessment of Intelligence

Personality Assessment

Behavioural and Cognitive Assessment

RESEARCH METHODS

EXPERIMENTAL METHODS

Controlled Experimental Research

Quasi-Experimental Methods

NONEXPERIMENTAL METHODS

Correlational Research

The Case Study

Single-Subject Research

Epidemiological Research

Studies of Inheritance

STATISTICAL VS. CLINICAL SIGNIFICANCE

ETHICAL CONSIDERATIONS

LEARNING OBJECTIVES

When you have completed your study of the chapter, you should be able to:

1. Discuss the difference between a diagnosis and an assessment.

2. Discuss the various ways of assessing a test's reliability and validity.

3. Compare the strengths and weaknesses of the clinical and actuarial approaches to prediction.

4. Describe the four brain imaging techniques described in the text, and comment on their usefulness.

5. Describe the Bender Visual-Motor Gestalt Test, and discuss its major drawback.

6. Explain the following subtests of the Halstead-Reitan neuropsychological test battery:

   Category test

   Rhythm test

   Tactual performance test

   Tapping test

   Grip strength test

   Auditory test

7. Describe the three types of clinical interview, explaining their advantages and disadvantages.

8. Briefly describe the abilities assessed by the Stanford-Binet Scales and the Wechsler Adult Intelligence Scale.

9. Describe each of the following projective tests:

   Rorschach inkblot test

   Thematic Apperception Test (TAT)

   Sentence Completion Test

10. Briefly describe each of the following personality inventories:

   Minnesota Multiphasic Personality Inventory (MMPI)

   Million Clinical Multiaxial Inventory (MCMI)

   Personality Assessment Inventory (PAI)

11. Contrast *in vivo* and *analogue* observations.

12. Describe what each of the letters in Kanfer and Phillips's SORC represents.

13. Explain how self-monitoring may be used in assessment.

14. Summarize the characteristics of a true experiment.

15. Explain how researchers control for placebo effects in experimental research.

16. Describe the two most important forms of validity in an experiment.

17. Discuss the pros and cons of experimental research.

18. Explain how quasi-experimental methods differ from experimental research.

19. Describe the three possible interpretations of the results of correlational research, and explain why we cannot establish cause-effect conclusions using this type of research.

20. Compare the idiographic and nomothetic approaches to research. Describe the advantages and disadvantages of each approach, and explain how this relates to the case-study approach.

21. Discuss the pros and cons of the ABAB design.

22. Define *incidence* and *prevalence*. Give an example where knowing each would be useful.

23. Explain what is meant by *cross-fostering*. Why is this a particularly strong method for investigating the genetic bases of disorders?

24. Discuss why it is important to avoid drawing conclusions regarding heritable traits when studying monozygotic (MZ) twins reared in the same family.

25. Discuss what is meant by the notions of statistical significance and clinical significance.

26. Briefly discuss four broad ethical principles—described in the Canadian Code of Ethics for Psychologists—that are related to teaching, research, assessment, and treatment.

KEY WORDS

Psychological assessment _____

_____

Test-retest reliability _____

_____

Alternate-form reliability _____

_____

Internal consistency _____

_____

Split-half reliability _____

_____

Coefficient alpha _____

_____

Face validity _____

_____

Content validity _____

_____

Criterion validity _____

_____

Construct validity _____

_____

Clinical approach _____

_____

Actuarial approach _____

_____

Computerized axial tomography (CAT) _____

_____

Magnetic resonance imaging (MRI) _____

_____

Positron emission tomography (PET) _____

_____

Bender Visual-Motor Gestalt Test _____

_____

Rapport _____

_____

Mental status examination _____

_____

Intelligence quotient (IQ) _____

_____

Stanford-Binet scales _____

_____

Wechsler Adult Intelligence Scale _____

_____

WAIS-III _____

_____

Projective test _____

_____

Rorschach inkblot test _____

_____

Exner system _____

_____

Thematic apperception test (TAT) _____

_____

Sentence completion test _____

_____

Minnesota Multiphasic Personality Inventory (MMPI) _____

_____

Millon Clinical Multiaxial Inventory (MCMI) _____

_____

Person by situation interaction _____

_____

In vivo observation _____

_____

Analogue observational setting _____

_____

Reactivity _____

_____

SORC _____

Description _____

_____

Science _____

_____

Experiment _____

_____

Random assignment _____

_____

Experimental group _____

_____

Independent variable _____

_____

Dependent variable _____

_____

Control group _____

_____

Experimental effect _____

_____

Pretest _____

_____

Post-test _____

_____

Placebo effect _____

_____

Placebo _____

_____

Double-blind _____

_____

Internal validity _____

_____

External validity _____

_____

Quasi-experimental study _____

_____

Confound _____

_____

Correlational method _____

_____

Longitudinal studies _____

_____

Case study _____

_____

Single-subject designs _____

_____

ABAB (or reversal design) _____

_____

Epidemiology _____

_____

Incidence _____

_____

Prevalence _____

_____

Proband _____

_____

Cross-fostering _____

_____

Monozygotic (MZ) twins _____

_____

Dizygotic (DZ) twins _____

_____

Statistical significance _____

_____

Clinical significance _____

_____

Normative comparison _____

_____

FILL-IN-THE-BLANKS

1. A _____ is only as good as the assessment on which it is based.

2. An _____ is only as good as the tools used to carry it out.

3. The _____ method of testing internal consistency involves determining the correlation between odd-numbered and even-numbered items in a test.

4. _____ validity refers to the importance of a test within a specific theoretical framework and can only be understood in the context of that framework.

5. The _____ approach to prediction involves unbiased, scientifically validated statistical procedures, empirical methods, and formal rules.

6. _____ is a noninvasive technique that involves producing a strong homogeneous magnetic field around the patient's head.

7. CAT scans have revealed that schizophrenics have smaller _____ lobes than controls.

8. _____ is a combination of computerized tomography and radioisotope imaging.

9. A child redrawing a four-sided figure, while taking the Bender Visual-Motor Gestalt Test, consistently extends her lines longer than is appropriate. This type of error is known as _____.

10. The tapping test is a subtest of the _____ neurological test battery.

11. In the _____ interview, although clinicians have considerable leeway about what questions to ask, they are guided by an outline listing the dimensions of the patient's functioning that must be covered.

12. Of all psychological traits, _____ shows the most stability.

13. _____ tests generally have their roots in psychoanalytic principles.

14. The _____ test is a projective test that involves constructing stories about pictures depicting ambiguous social interactions.

15. The _____ in the MMPI-2 measures a respondent's tendency to claim excessive virtue or to present an overall favourable image.

16. Whereas the MMPI-2 focuses mainly on Axis I disorders in the DSM, the _____ was developed to help clinicians make judgments within the multiaxial DSM system, especially in the personality disorders found on Axis II.

17. Two behavioural and cognitive observational techniques described in the text include the _____ and the _____.

18. A _____ can be a very important tool used to track behaviours in a self-monitoring program.

19. The experimental group in an experiment is administered the _____ variable.

20. The _____ effect refers to changes resulting from a research participant's expectations of improvement, or reports of improvement to please the experimenter.

21. The _____ method is the oldest approach to the study of abnormal behaviour and has been extensively used by clinicians to describe patients they have treated.

22. Whereas _____ refers to the number of new cases of a disorder in a particular population over a specified time period, _____ is the frequency of a disorder in a population at a given point in time.

23. _____ twins result from the fertilization by a single sperm of a single ovum.

MULTIPLE CHOICE

1. An assessment

   a. may have a purpose not related to a diagnosis
   b. is made up of several diagnoses
   c. must always be used toward making a diagnosis
   d. is almost always an unstructured interview

2. Test-retest reliability

   a. refers to the likelihood that a test's items correlate well to each other
   b. is only important in the field of education
   c. may be determined by calculating coefficient alpha
   d. refers to the degree to which a test yields the same results when given again to the same person

3. The extent to which a test's items resemble the characteristics associated with the concept being tested reflects its

    a. construct validity
    b. criterion validity
    c. face validity
    d. all of the above

4. An electroencephalogram (EEG) would be most useful in detecting

    a. depression
    b. obsessive-compulsive disorders
    c. schizophrenia
    d. seizure disorders

5. Right temporal lobe functioning is best indicated by the _____ subtest of the Halstead-Reitan neuropsychological battery.

    a. rhythm test
    b. tactual performance test
    c. category test
    d. auditory test

6. The most frequently used semistructured interview is the

    a. SCID
    b. mental status examination
    c. Luria-Nebraska
    d. MMPI

7. Which of the following dimensions is not assessed by the mental status examination?

    a. appearance
    b. affect
    c. social support
    d. behaviour

8. The first widely accepted and successful test of intelligence was designed by

    a. Alfred Binet
    b. Francis Galton
    c. David Wechsler
    d. none of the above

9. The most important types of validity to consider in a controlled experiment are

    a. criterion and internal
    b. construct and internal
    c. internal and external
    d. criterion and construct

10. A controlled experiment

    a. is relatively easy and inexpensive to implement
    b. is an ideographic approach rich in detail
    c. allows cause and effect to be established
    d. is highly biased by the clinician's perspective

11. In an experiment the _____ is measured to reveal any changes brought about by the _____.

    a. independent variable, dependent variable
    b. treatment group, independent variable
    c. control group, dependent variable
    d. dependent variable, independent variable

12. A confound occurs when

    a. one variable serves to negatively affect another variable
    b. two or more variables exert their influence at the same time
    c. the control group is aware that they are not being given the treatment
    d. participants drop out of an experiment

13. The correlational method

    a. is often used where experimental manipulation is impossible or unethical
    b. involves correlating the changes in the control and experimental method
    c. is usually quite expensive
    d. is a highly controlled procedure

14. A study revealed a high positive correlation between number of convicted offences and sensation-seeking in a criminal population. From this information we may accurately conclude that

    a. high sensation-seeking in criminals will likely lead to being caught and convicted
    b. a third factor is responsible for the noticed relationship between the two variables
    c. individuals who are high sensation-seekers commit more crimes and thus, while perhaps not getting caught more frequently than normal controls, still have a high rate of conviction
    d. none of the above

15. A study compared a group of students who suffered from test anxiety to another group who did not report anxiety. The participants in the two groups were similar in terms of age and gender. A personality inventory was administered to determine whether there were specific personality characteristics present in the anxiety group, but not present in the controls. This is an example of a(n) _____ study.

    a. correlational
    b. quasi-experimental
    c. epidemiological
    d. longitudinal

16. A reversal design involves

    a. reversing the order of treatments
    b. reversing back to baseline after treatment
    c. switching a participant from the treatment group to the control group
    d. none of the above

17. _____ would indicate the number of new cases of a disorder in a population over a year.

    a. Criterion validity
    b. Prevalence
    c. Trends
    d. Incidence

18. The percentage of genes shared in common between a proband and his/her niece or nephew is approximately

    a. 25%
    b. 12.5%
    c. 50%
    d. 5%

19. Cross-fostering involves

    a. adopted children whose biological parents have no disorder and whose adoptive parents have a disorder
    b. adopted children whose biological parents have a disorder and whose adoptive parents demonstrate no psychopathology
    c. a and b
    d. none of the above

20. Normative comparison involves

    a. determining whether or not an individual adheres to social norms
    b. statistically comparing an individual's test scores with a bank of scores collected from other individuals within the same population
    c. comparing treatment results to nondisturbed samples
    d. none of the above

ANSWERS

FILL-IN-THE-BLANKS

1. diagnosis
2. assessment
3. split-half
4. construct
5. actuarial
6. magnetic resonance imaging (MRI)
7. frontal
8. positron emission tomography (PET)
9. perseveration
10. Halstead-Reitan
11. semistructured
12. IQ
13. projective
14. TAT
15. Lie scale
16. Millon Clinical Multiaxial Inventory (MCMI)
17. Child Behaviour Checklist; Home Situations Questionnaire
18. diary
19. independent
20. placebo
21. case study
22. incidence; prevalence
23. monozygotic (MZ)

MULTIPLE CHOICE

1.	a	11.	d
2.	d	12.	b
3.	c	13.	a
4.	d	14.	d
5.	a	15.	b
6.	b	16.	b
7.	c	17.	d
8.	a	18.	a
9.	c	19.	b
10.	c	20.	c

CHAPTER 5

Anxiety Disorders

CHAPTER OUTLINE

Problem Solving

Relaxation

Other Techniques

TREATMENT EFFICACY

Treatment of Panic Disorder

Treatment of Specific Phobias

Treatment of Social Phobia

Treatment of Obsessive-Compulsive Disorder

Treatment of Posttraumatic Stress Disorder

Treatment of Generalized Anxiety Disorder

Comment on Treatments That Work

LEARNING OBJECTIVES

When you have completed your study of the chapter, you should be able to:

1. Distinguish among three distinctive components of emotion: physiological, cognitive, and behavioural.

2. Explain the differences between anxiety, fear, and panic.

3. Discuss the role of genetic factors in the etiology of anxiety disorders.

4. Describe the neural fear circuit underlying anxiety and underlying panic.

5. Explain Mowrer's two-factor theory of fear and anxiety, and discuss its shortcomings.

6. Discuss how cognitive models explain fear and anxiety.

7. Explain how parents and parenting style can play a role in the development of anxiety.

8. Describe the DMS-IV-TR diagnostic criteria for a diagnosis of panic attack.

9. Describe the characteristics of agoraphobia.

10. Explain how behavioural and psychophysiological strategies are used to assess panic.

11. Summarize how cognitive theories explain panic disorder.

12. Identify and describe five subtypes of specific phobias outlined in the DMS-IV-TR.

13. Explain how associative and nonassociative models account for the development of specific phobias.

14. Discuss what is meant by *biological preparedness*. Explain how this phenomenon may be related to the etiology of specific phobias.

15. Discuss what is meant by *disgust sensitivity*. Explain how this phenomenon may be related to the etiology of specific phobias.

16. Describe the DMS-IV-TR diagnostic criteria for social phobia.

17. Discuss the strategies socially phobic individuals use to reduce anxiety.

18. Describe two prototypical profiles of social phobia onset.

19. Explain the role of genetics and of early psychosocial experiences in the development of social phobia.

20. Discuss the role of cognitive factors and abnormal social information processing in social phobia.

21. Differentiate between obsessions, compulsions, and neutralizations, providing examples of each.

22. Explain what is meant by *thought-action-fusion* (TAF), providing examples of different types of TAF.

23. Describe the DSM-IV-TR diagnostic criteria for obsessive-compulsive disorder.

24. Describe four subtypes of obsessive-compulsive disorder.

25. Explain how neurobiological factors may be involved in OCD.

26. Describe how cognitive-behavioural approaches conceptualize OCD.

27. Describe the DMS-IV-TR diagnostic criteria for posttraumatic stress disorder (PTSD).

28. Explain how PTSD differs from all other anxiety disorders.

29. Describe the differences in how traumatic memories and non-traumatic memories are stored, according to Dual Representation Theory. What implications do these differences have for therapy?

30. Describe the DMS-IV-TR diagnostic criteria for generalized anxiety disorder (GAD).

31. Discuss the role of worry in GAD.

32. Identify and discuss the benefits and shortcomings of each of the various psychopharmacological treatments for anxiety disorders.

33. Discuss the rationale underlying cognitive restructuring interventions. Identify and describe three strategies commonly used in such interventions.

34. Discuss the rationale underlying exposure as an intervention technique. Identify and describe four well-known exposure techniques.

35. Discuss the use of each of the following therapy techniques:

    Response prevention

    Problem solving

    Relaxation

36. Briefly discuss the efficacy of treatments used with each of the following disorders:

    Panic disorder

    Specific phobias

    Social phobia

    Obsessive-compulsive disorder

    Posttraumatic stress disorder

    Generalized anxiety disorder

KEY WORDS

Anxiety _____

_____

Fear _____

_____

Fight or flight response _____

_____

Panic _____

_____

Neurosis _____

_____

Two-factor theory _____

_____

Vicarious learning _____

_____

Panic attack _____

_____

Agoraphobia _____

_____

Behavioural avoidance test (BAT) _____

_____

Catastrophic misinterpretation _____

_____

Anxiety sensitivity _____

_____

Alarm theory _____

_____

Illness phobia _____

_____

Equipotentiality premise _____

_____

Nonassociative model _____

_____

Biological preparedness _____

_____

Disgust sensitivity _____

_____

Obsessions _____

_____

Compulsions _____

_____

Neutralizations _____

_____

Thought-action fusion _____

_____

Emotional numbing _____

_____

Intolerance of uncertainty _____

_____

Systematic desensitization _____

_____

Fear hierarchy _____

_____

In vivo exposure _____

_____

Flooding (intense exposure) _____

_____

Interoceptive exposure _____

_____

Response prevention _____

_____

Worry exposure _____

_____

Worry behaviour prevention _____

_____

Subtle avoidance _____

_____

FILL-IN-THE-BLANKS

1. Anxiety is an affective state whereby an individual feels _____ by the potential occurrence of a future negative event.

2. Compared to anxiety, fear is more _____-oriented.

3. Whereas _____ is an emotional response to an objective, current, and identifiable event, _____ is an extreme fear reaction that is triggered even though there is nothing to be afraid of.

4. The neural fear circuit begins with the registry of sensory information at the _____, which is then sent to parts of the _____.

5. _____ are a class of anti-anxiety medications that operate primarily on GABA-mediated inhibition of the fear system.

6. In 1947, Mowrer proposed his _____ theory, which attempted to account for the acquisition of fears and the maintenance of anxiety.

7. According to DSM-IV-TR, a panic attack must occur suddenly, reaching a peak within _____ minutes.

8. Most people who develop panic disorder do so in _____ to _____ adulthood.

9. Women are _____ as likely to be affected by panic disorder than are men.

10. The cardinal feature of panic disorder is that patients initially experience _____ panic attacks and have marked apprehension and worry over the possibility of having additional attacks.

11. There are a number of medical conditions, such as _____ and _____, that create symptoms that mimic panic disorder.

12. Cognitive theories focus on the idea that individuals with panic disorder tend to catastrophically _____ common bodily sensations, such as dizziness, shortness of breath, increased heart rate, and so on.

13. Barlow and his colleagues have proposed an _____ theory of panic, where individuals develop apprehension over experiencing further panic attacks and focus intensely on their bodily sensations to prepare for and prevent future attacks.

14. Whereas fears are adaptive reactions to threats, _____ are excessive and unrealistic fear reactions.

15. One of the main criticisms of the classical conditioning model of fear is that it assumes that all neutral stimuli have an equal potential of becoming phobias, a notion known as the _____ premise.

16. In terms of prevalence, _____ is the third most prevalent psychiatric disorder, second only to depression and alcohol-related disorders.

17. _____ are recurrent and uncontrollable thoughts, impulses, or ideas that the individual finds disturbing and anxiety-provoking.

18. _____ are behavioural or mental acts that are used by individuals to try to prevent, cancel, or "undo" the feared consequences and distress caused by an obsession.

19. Trying to suppress obsessional thoughts can have the paradoxical effect of increasing their frequency, a phenomenon known as the _____ effect.

20. A central diagnostic feature of PTSD that distinguishes it from other anxiety disorders is that upon being reminded of the traumatic event, the individual _____ the event in some way.

21. _____ are currently the most well-used and effective medications for the treatment of anxiety disorders.

22. Despite their significant potential adverse effects, _____ are the most effective pharmacological interventions in the treatment of social phobia.

23. _____ are the most well-prescribed anxiolitic medications.

24. One of the earliest forms of exposure was _____, initially developed by Joseph Wolpe.

25. Exposure to bodily sensations, useful in the treatment of panic disorder, is referred to as _____.

26. The main form of psychological treatment for specific phobias is _____

27. The main psychological treatment for obsessive-compulsive disorder has involved _____ and _____.

28. Studies show that _____ medication is effective in reducing 65 to 70 percent of the symptoms of generalized anxiety disorder in the short term, although the long-term outcome data are not encouraging.

MULTIPLE CHOICE

1. In the 18th century, people who were not psychotic but still had emotional problems were labelled
   a. mad
   b. phobic
   c. hysteric
   d. neurotic

2. Individuals who have a family member who suffers from an anxiety disorder are _____ more likely to have an anxiety disorder than are those without a family history.

   a. one to two times
   b. four to six times
   c. seven to nine times
   d. at least 10 times

3. As a young child, Melissa was bitten by a dog and developed an intense fear of dogs. She has never again been bitten, yet her fear remains strong. According to the two-factor model, Melissa's fear of dogs does not extinguish because

   a. she constantly relives the initial trauma of the experience
   b. she maintains a high level of disgust sensitivity
   c. she avoids dogs as a means of reducing anxiety
   d. she tries to neutralize her anxiety by means of compulsive actions or thoughts

4. Melissa's fear of dogs was likely initially acquired via _____ conditioning; however, her fear of dogs is maintained through a process of _____ conditioning.

   a. classical, operant
   b. prepared, classical
   c. classical, prepared
   d. operant, prepared

5. Dave was with Melissa when she was initially bitten. Despite the fact that he was not bitten himself, Dave acquired an intense fear of dogs simply by watching what happened to Melissa. Such learning is referred to as

   a. prepared
   b. operant
   c. vicarious
   d. nonassociative

6. Anxiety about being in places or situations where an individual might find it difficult to escape is referred to as

    a. anxiety sensitivity
    b. agoraphobia
    c. catastrophic potentiality
    d   behavioural avoidance anxiety

7. Although higher cortical areas are not directly involved in the neural fear circuit, they are necessary for _____ conditioned fears.

    a. eliciting
    b. acquiring
    c. precipitating
    d. extinguishing

8. Panic disorder tends to run in families. The biological relatives of people with panic disorder are _____ times more likely to develop panic disorder than are individuals who do not have panic-prone relatives.

    a. 5
    b. 10
    c. 12–15
    d. 15–20

9. Seligman argued that the process of natural selection has equipped humans with the predisposition to fear objects and situations that represented threats to our species. This notion, referred to as _____, suggests that people are more likely to learn to fear certain stimuli than others.

    a. the non-equipotentiality premise
    b. biological preparedness
    c. a nonassociative model
    d. the pre-wired fear principle

10. Individuals with social phobia tend to be high in _____, which refers to the awareness of oneself as an object of attention, or the tendency to see one's actions from the perspective of an outside observer.

    a. public arousability
    b. social anxiety sensitivity
    c. public self-consciousness
    d. behavioural avoidance

11. Which of the following is *not* true about social phobia?

    a. Genetic factors appear to account for approximately one-half the variance in risk for social phobia.

    b. A majority of individuals suffering from social phobia report having been bullied or severely teased during childhood.

    c. Most individuals with this disorder develop their social phobias early in childhood.

    d. Like agoraphobic individuals, people with social phobia often experience anxiety in public places.

12. Which of the following is *not* characteristic of obsessions?

    a. controllable   b. persistent

    c. distressing   d. anxiety-provoking

13. Repetitive behaviours or cognitive acts that are intended to reduce anxiety are referred to as

    a. obsessions   b. neutralizations

    c. compulsions   d. numbing rituals

14. Thought-action-fusion is related to obsessive-compulsive symptoms. Such thinking also occurs, however, in non-OCD students. Only the _____ form of TAF is considered to be a pathological OCD belief.

    a. Likelihood-Self

    b. Moral

    c. Likelihood-Enhancing

    d. Likelihood-Other

15. Which of the following is characteristic of posttraumatic stress disorder?

    a. recurrent re-experiencing of the traumatic event

    b. avoidance of trauma-related stimuli and numbing of general responsiveness

    c. persistent symptoms of increased arousal

    d. all of the above

16. Both generalized anxiety disorder and major depressive disorder share several diagnostic features, such as concentration difficulties, irritability, ruminations, and so on. A key difference between the two is that anxious thinking tends to be focused on _____ threat, whereas depressed thinking is focused on _____ losses or failures.

    a. supposed; real   b. future; past

    c. evolutionarily significant; neutral   d. real; supposed

17. Dave has recurrent concerns about the accuracy of his work as an accountant. Often he will agonize over whether he correctly completed a client's taxes, ruminating about the consequences of possible errors. He often checks and rechecks his calculations and seeks reassurance from his clients that they are satisfied with his work. Dave most likely would be diagnosed as suffering from

    a. generalized anxiety disorder
    b. posttraumatic stress disorder
    c. obsessive compulsive disorder
    d. social phobia

18. Meg has a perpetual feeling that something catastrophic is about to happen to her. She tends to think through her activities in detail, focusing on potential negative events that could happen. When her friends tell her "Oh, don't worry so much!" she replies, "How can you tell me not to worry? Do you want something bad to happen to me?" Meg would most likely be diagnosed as suffering from

    a. generalized anxiety disorder
    b. specific phobia
    c. obsessive compulsive disorder
    d. social phobia

19. Individuals with anxiety problems often

    a. overestimate the probability and severity of various threats (risk) and underestimate their ability for coping with them (resources)
    b. are so preoccupied with their own anxiety that they tend to minimize the severity of various threats in their environment
    c. tend to be mostly preoccupied with past failures and shortcomings and spend little time focusing on the future
    d. are equally concerned with threats in the past and the future

20. The most popular psychological treatment for social anxiety disorder is

    a. worry exposure
    b. response prevention
    c. worry behaviour prevention
    d. cognitive-behaviour group therapy

ANSWERS

FILL-IN-THE-BLANKS

1. threatened
2. present
3. fear; panic
4. thalamus; amygdala
5. benzodiazepines
6. two-factor
7. 10
8. early; middle
9. twice
10. uncued
11. hypoglycemia; hyperthyroidism
12. misinterpret
13. alarm
14. phobias
15. equipotentiality
16. social phobia
17. obsessions
18. neutralizations
19. rebound
20. re-experiences
21. antidepressant drugs
22. monoamine oxidase inhibitors
23. SSRIs
24. systematic desensitization
25. interoceptive exposure
26. in vivo exposure
27. exposure; response prevention
28. benzodiazepine

MULTIPLE CHOICE

1.	d	11.	c
2.	b	12.	a
3.	c	13.	c
4.	a	14.	d
5.	c	15.	d
6.	b	16.	b
7.	d	17.	c
8.	a	18.	a
9.	b	19.	a
10.	c	20.	d

CHAPTER 6

Dissociative and Somatoform Disorders

CHAPTER OUTLINE

BODY DYSMORPHIC DISORDER

ETIOLOGY

TREATMENT

LEARNING OBJECTIVES

When you have completed your study of the chapter, you should be able to:

1. Briefly describe each of the following dissociative disorders:

   Dissociative amnesia

   Dissociative fugue

   Depersonalization disorder

   Dissociative identity disorder (DID)

2. Compare five patterns of memory loss described in DSM-IV-TR.

3. Discuss the debate concerning repressed memories and false memories.

4. Discuss the importance and significance of physical and sexual abuse in DID patients.

5. Discuss the effectiveness of psychotherapy, hypnosis, and medication in treating DID.

6. Describe the major symptoms of each of the following somatoform disorders:

   Somatization disorder

Conversion disorder

Pain disorder

Hypochondriasis

Body dysmorphic disorder

7. Explain how conversion disorder differs from true neurological problems.

8. Describe the difference between somatization disorder and hypochondriasis.

9. Describe the differences between malingering and factitious disorder.

10. Discuss the treatment options available for somatoform disorders.

KEY WORDS

Hysteria _____

_____

Dissociative disorders _____

_____

Dissociation _____

_____

Dissociative amnesia _____

Dissociative fugue _____

_____

Repressed _____

_____

False memory syndrome _____

_____

Depersonalization _____

_____

Depersonalization disorder _____

_____

Derealization _____

_____

Dissociative identity disorder (DID) _____

_____

Alter _____

_____

Switching _____

_____

Somatoform disorders _____

_____

Malingering _____

_____

Factitious disorders _____

_____

Somatization disorder _____

_____

Conversion disorder _____

_____

Glove anaesthesia _____

_____

La belle indifference _____

_____

Pain disorder _____

_____

Hypochondriasis _____

_____

Body dysmorphic disorder _____

_____

FILL-IN-THE-BLANKS

1. The dissociative disorders and some of the somatic disorders were once viewed as expressions of _____, a term that dates back to ancient Greece.

2. The primary symptom of _____ is the inability to verbally recall significant personal information in the absence of organic impairment.

3. The following five patterns of memory loss are described in DSM-IV-TR: (1)_____ amnesia describes the failure to recall information during a very specific time period. (2) _____ amnesia involves recalling only parts of a trauma, while the rest is forgotten. (3) _____ amnesia is the inability to remember an individual's

entire life. (4) _____ amnesia is the inability to remember information from a specific date until the present. (5) _____ amnesia involves forgetting certain categories of information.

4. In sexual abuse cases, defence lawyers sometimes rebuke evidence from psychologists pertaining to lost memories by making reference to _____ syndrome.

5. _____ is an extremely rare condition where individuals forget who they are and may even travel thousands of miles from home before they recall their personal history.

6. Suddenly feeling like a robot who is able to respond to those nearby but without feeling connected to one's actions is called _____.

7. Unlike other dissociative disorders, there is no _____ impairment or _____ confusion in depersonalization disorder.

8. The process of changing from one personality to another is referred to as _____.

9. In dissociative identity disorder, typically one personality is identified as the host, while subsequent personalities are identified as _____.

10. Some researchers argue that DID is likely an _____ condition caused by the suggestions of an overzealous clinician to a susceptible patient.

11. Although there is concern regarding its use because of the potential of retrieving confabulated personalities, _____ continues to be a popular treatment for dissociative identity disorder.

12. Patients suffering from conversion disorder often display indifference or a lack of worry—referred to as _____—about their symptoms.

13. _____ often leads to "doctor shopping."

14. The term _____ refers to the condition in which an individual deliberately adopts the sick role and complains of symptoms to achieve some specific objective, such as receiving insurance money or avoiding an exam.

15. Individuals with _____ deliberately fake or generate symptoms in order to gain their doctor's attention or to assume the role of the patient.

MULTIPLE CHOICE

1. Failure to recall information during a very specific period of time is called _____ amnesia.

    a. localized
    b. generalized
    c. continuous
    d. none of the above

2. Assuming a new identity and leaving familiar surroundings are characteristics of

    a. dissociative amnesia
    b. dissociative fugue
    c. dissociative identity disorder
    d. depersonalization disorder

3. Feeling detached from one's self or surroundings is characteristic of

    a. dissociative amnesia
    b. dissociative fugue
    c. dissociative identity disorder
    d. depersonalization disorder

4. Feelings of depersonalization

    a. are involved in switching from one alter to another
    b. are sometimes described as *la belle indifference*
    c. involve severe disturbances or alterations of identity, memory, and consciousness
    d. are a relatively common experience

5. Unlike other dissociative disorders, there is no memory impairment or identity confusion in

    a. depersonalization disorder
    b. somatization disorder
    c. dissociative fugue
    d. body dysmorphic disorder

6. For dissociative identity disorder to be diagnosed, there must be

    a. at least two distinct personality states that exert control over the person's behaviour
    b. sexual and/or physical abuse during childhood
    c. no connection between the alters
    d. all of the above

7. Dr. Nick Spanos proposed that DID is

   a. a legitimate diagnosis
   b. intentionally caused by practitioners
   c. produced by role-playing
   d. none of the above

8. In dissociative identity disorder, typically one personality is identified as _____, while subsequent personalities are identified as alters.

   a. central
   b. host
   c. senior
   d. primary

9. Switching refers to

   a. the process of changing from one personality to another
   b. faking symptoms that repeatedly change so that the physician is baffled by the presenting problem
   c. the patient's preoccupation with symptoms that change over the course of time
   d. changing between being worried and being unconcerned about physical problems

10. Which medication is sometimes used to help the individual with DID recall previously forgotten memories or identify additional alters?

    a. methylphenidate   b. sodium amytal
    c. methadone   d. none of the above

11. To meet DSM-IV-TR diagnostic criteria for somatization disorder, the individual must complain of

    a. pain symptoms during at least four bodily functions
    b. two gastrointestinal symptoms other than pain
    c. two sexual symptoms
    d. four pain symptoms at three different sites

12. Adopting the sick role in order to achieve a specific objective, such as avoiding an exam, is called

    a. factitious disorder
    b. somatoform disorder
    c. hypochondriasis
    d. malingering

13. In _____, symptoms are located in voluntary motor and sensory functions that suggest neurological or other medical etiologies, but these cannot be confirmed.

    a. somatization disorder
    b. conversion disorder
    c. hypochondriasis
    d. pain disorder

14. Jane is intensely dissatisfied with the shape of her nose. Although her friends cannot see what the supposed problem is, Jane spends hundreds of hours examining her face, focusing on perceived defects in her nose. She is now considering plastic surgery to correct the "defect." This excessive preoccupation with an imagined defect is referred to as

    a. *la belle indifference*   b. a factitious disorder
    c. body dysmorphic disorder   d. hypochondriasis

15. In conversion disorder, the more medically naive a person, the more _____ will be the presenting symptoms.

    a. predictable
    b. sophisticated
    c. original
    d. implausible

16. Body dysmorphic disorder usually begins

    a. in early childhood
    b. in the mid-twenties
    c. in adolescence
    d. in the post-retirement years

17. Individuals with body dysmorphic disorder

    a. spend considerable effort trying to control their preoccupation with their appearance
    b. describe their preoccupation with their appearance as a major source of discomfort
    c. refuse to think about or discuss their appearance with others
    d. often are cured only by plastic surgery

18. Long-standing fears, suspicions, and worries about having a serious illness, despite medical reassurance to the contrary, are associated with

    a. *la belle indifference*   b. malingering
    c. factitious disorders   d. hypochondriasis

ANSWERS

FILL-IN-THE-BLANKS

1. hysteria
2. dissociative amnesia
3. localized; selective; generalized; continuous; systematized
4. false memory
5. dissociative fugue
6. depersonalization
7. memory; identity
8. switching
9. alters
10. iatrogenic
11. hypnosis
12. *la belle indifference*
13. hypochondriasis
14. malingering
15. factitious disorders

MULTIPLE CHOICE

1. a	10. b
2. b	11. b
3. d	12. d
4. d	13. b
5. a	14. c
6. a	15. d
7. c	16. c
8. b	17. b
9. a	18. d

CHAPTER 7

Psychophysiological Disorders

CHAPTER OUTLINE

LEARNING OBJECTIVES

When you have completed your study of the chapter, you should be able to:

1. Distinguish between the terms *behavioural medicine* and *health psychology*.

2. Explain the differences between the terms *illness* and *disease*.

3. Describe the sequence of organs and effects that make up the hypothalamic-pituitary-adrenal-cortical (HPA) axis.

4. Explain the functions of the sympathetic and parasympathetic branches of the autonomic nervous system.

5. Describe the three general categories of immune response—nonspecific, cellular, and humoral.

6. Outline the three phases that Hans Selye proposed make up the general adaptation syndrome.

7. Distinguish between what Richard Lazarus refers to as primary appraisal and secondary appraisal, in his transactional model of stress.

8. Discuss how social status may influence health.

9. Explain how controllability can influence the effects of stressful events.

10. Discuss how social support may influence the effects of stressful events.

11. Explain what ulcers are, and discuss how researchers have examined whether stress causes ulcers.

12. Outline four criteria that may be used to determine whether a psychological variable plays a causal role in the development of disease.

13. Describe how researchers have investigated physiological consequences of marital conflict.

14. Briefly describe the processes involved in cardiovascular disease.

15. Describe how both cardiovascular factors and psychosocial factors can contribute to the development of cardiovascular disease.

16. Describe the Type A behaviour pattern, and explain how it is related to heart disease.

17. Briefly outline the five possible models that Timothy Smith suggests may link health risk with hostility.

18. Discuss what researchers have found concerning the relationship between depression and cardiovascular disease.

19. Discuss the various psychosocial strategies that have been used in the treatment of psychophysiological disorders.

KEY WORDS

Dualistic _____

_____

Behavioural medicine _____

_____

Health psychology _____

_____

Mechanism _____

_____

Lesion _____

_____

Nonspecific immune responses _____

_____

Cellular immunity _____

_____

Humoral immunity _____

_____

Psychoneuroimmunology _____

_____

Alarm _____

Resistance _____

Exhaustion_____

General adaptation syndrome _____

Transactional model _____

Appraisal _____

Primary appraisal _____

Secondary appraisal _____

Internal locus of control _____

External locus of control _____

Longitudinal study _____

Ischemic heart disease _____

Myocardial infarction _____

_____

Stroke _____

_____

Potential years of life lost (PYLL) _____

_____

Vasculature _____

_____

Systolic blood pressure _____

_____

Diastolic blood pressure _____

_____

Cardiac output_____

_____

Total peripheral resistance _____

_____

Arrhythmia _____

_____

Atherosclerosis _____

_____

Atherogenesis_____

_____

Controllable risk factors _____

_____

Protective factors _____

_____

Hypertension _____

_____

Stress reactivity paradigm_____

_____

Cardiovascular reactivity _____

_____

Type A _____

_____

Psychophysiological reactivity model _____

_____

Psychosocial vulnerability model_____

_____

Transactional model _____

_____

Health behaviour model _____

_____

Constitutional vulnerability _____

_____

FILL-IN-THE-BLANKS

1. The term _____ refers to any application of psychological methods and theories to understand the origins of disease, individual responses to disease, and the dimensions and determinants of good health.

2. Whereas illness is marked by _____, disease is marked by _____.

3. The branch of the autonomic nervous system that "applies the brakes" and returns the body to a more quiescent state is the _____ nervous system.

4. The general adaptation syndrome consists of three phases: _____, _____, and _____.

5. According to Richard Lazarus, stress is neither a property of stimulus nor of response, but rather an ongoing series of _____ between individuals and their environments.

6. People who have an _____ locus of control see themselves as the masters of their own destiny, whereas those with an _____ locus of control see themselves as being buffeted by the random events of the world.

7. Karasek et al. proposed a job strain model that characterizes occupations on two dimensions: _____ demand and _____ control.

8. An _____ is an erosion in the lining of the stomach or duodenum.

9. In a _____ study, a large group of people are evaluated with respect to the existence of psychological or behavioural features and are then followed up, often years or decades later, to determine whether they have developed a disease.

10. Diseases of the _____ system are the leading causes of death and disability in Western societies.

11. Blood pressure is a consequence of two major variables: _____ (the amount of blood pumped by the heart) and _____ (the diameter of the blood vessels).

12. Disturbances in the normal pumping rhythm of the heart are referred to as _____.

13. _____ is a disease state that consists of a build-up of plaques on the walls of the blood vessels.

14. According to the _____ model, proposed by Timothy Smith, hostile people are at higher risk for various diseases because they experience exaggerated autonomic and neuroendocrine responses during stress.

MULTIPLE CHOICE

1. The term _____ refers to the application of the methods of behaviour modification to the treatment or prevention of disease.

   a. health psychology
   b. psychoneuroimmunology
   c. behavioural medicine
   d. transactional model

2. When the HPA axis is activated, the pituitary gland secretes a substance called _____ into the bloodstream.

   a. cortisol
   b. adrenocorticotrophic hormone
   c. glucocorticoid
   d. adrenaline

3. Increased blood pressure, heart rate, and perspiration, as well as decreased digestive activity follow when

   a. the sympathetic nervous system is aroused
   b. the parasympathetic nervous system is aroused
   c. the immune system is aroused
   d. all of the above

4. Cellular immunity is based on the action of a class of blood cells called

   a. B-lymphocytes
   b. granulocytes
   c. monocytes
   d. T-lymphocytes

5. Exposure of subjects to acute stressors in a laboratory setting, such as making them perform an extemporaneous speech,

   a. consistently produces changes in immune system function, such as increased numbers of killer and suppressor T-cells and reduced T-cell proliferation
   b. consistently produces changes in immune system function, such as reduced numbers of killer and suppressor T-cells and increased T-cell proliferation
   c. has little effect on immune system function, although it clearly influences autonomic nervous system activity
   d. none of the above

6. During which phase of the general adaptation syndrome does the body actively fight or cope with a stressor through immune system and neuroendocrine changes?

   a. alarm
   b. resistance
   c. exhaustion
   d. appraisal

7. When faced with an event that may have adaptational significance, the individual unconsciously poses the following question: "Is this a threat to me?" In Richard Lazarus's view this evaluative process is called

   a. problem-focused coping   b. emotion-focused coping
   c. primary appraisal   d. secondary appraisal

8. If, in the situation above, the individual concludes that there is a threat, then a further set of _____ takes place, involving the metaphoric question, "Is there anything I can do about this?"

   a. problem-focused coping   b. emotion-focused coping
   c. primary appraisals   d. secondary appraisals

9. High strain jobs tend to involve

   a. high demands and low control
   b. low demands and high control
   c. high demands and high control
   d. low demands and low control

10. Hill has outlined a number of criteria that may be applied in order to evaluate whether a psychological variable plays a causal role in illness and disease. Which of these criteria are commonly established by means of longitudinal studies?

   a. association   b. precedence
   c. consistency   d. strength of association

11. In Canada, heart disease and stroke account for approximately _____% of deaths per year.

   a. 12   b. 27
   c. 41   d. 73

12. Blood pressure is commonly expressed in two numbers in the following sequence:

   a. systolic blood pressure/diastolic blood pressure
   b. cardiac output/total peripheral resistance
   c. diastolic blood pressure/systolic blood pressure
   d. total peripheral resistance/cardiac output

13. Activation of components of the sympathetic nervous system affecting _____ receptors on the heart will speed up the rate at which the heart beats.

   a. catecholamine   b. helper-T
   c. alpha-adrenergic   d. beta-adrenergic

14. High blood cholesterol and cigarette smoking are considered major _____ for cardiovascular disease.

   a. stressors
   b. protective factors
   c. coping strategies
   d. controllable risk factors

15. Hypertension for which a simple cause cannot be identified is referred to as

   a. controllable
   b. preventable
   c. essential
   d. generic

16. Which of the following statements about Type A behaviour and heart disease is supported by research?

   a. Risk associated with Type A behaviour is highly related to other risk factors, such as smoking.
   b. All the components of the Type A pattern of behaviour are equally likely to lead to heart disease.
   c. People diagnosed as Type A are approximately twice as likely as others to die of heart disease.
   d. all of the above

17. Which of the following is least likely to be related to heart disease?

   a. the tendency to respond with anger and contempt
   b. the tendency to view other people with cynicism and to impute bad intentions to others
   c. reporting that one is extremely busy and pressured at work
   d. direct and subtle aggressiveness and antagonism

18. Timothy Smith has outlined five possible models explaining how hostility leads to health risk. The psychosocial vulnerability model suggests that

   a. hostile people experience exaggerated autonomic and neuroendocrine responses during stress
   b. hostile people may be more likely to engage in unhealthy behaviours
   c. hostile people experience a more demanding interpersonal life than others
   d. hostile people have a constitutional vulnerability to health problems

ANSWERS

FILL-IN-THE-BLANKS

1. health psychology
2. symptoms; signs
3. parasympathetic
4. alarm; resistance; exhaustion
5. transactions
6. internal; external
7. psychological; decision
8. ulcer
9. longitudinal
10. cardiovascular
11. cardiac output; total peripheral resistance
12. arrhythmias
13. atherosclerosis
14. psychophysiological reactivity

MULTIPLE CHOICE

1.	c	10.	b
2.	b	11.	c
3.	a	12.	a
4.	d	13.	d
5.	a	14.	d
6.	b	15.	c
7.	c	16.	c
8.	d	17.	c
9.	a	18.	c

CHAPTER 8

Mood Disorders and Suicide

CHAPTER OUTLINE

HISTORICAL PERSPECTIVE

DIAGNOSTIC ISSUES

UNIPOLAR MOOD DISORDERS

MAJOR DEPRESSIVE DISORDER

Diagnostic Specifiers

Prevalence and Course

Underdiagnosis

Comorbidity

DYSTHYMIC DISORDER

BIPOLAR MOOD DISORDERS

Mania

Bipolar I and Bipolar II

Cyclothymia

Rapid Cycling Depression/Mania

SEASONAL AFFECTIVE DISORDER

MOOD DISORDER WITH POSTPARTUM ONSET

PSYCHOLOGICAL THEORIES

Psychodynamic Attachment

Cognitive Models

LEARNING OBJECTIVES

When you have completed your study of the chapter, you should be able to:

1. Differentiate between unipolar disorders and bipolar disorders.

2. Describe the symptoms, prevalence, and course of major depressive disorder.

3. Explain the similarities and differences between dysthymic disorder and major depression.

4. Describe the characteristics of bipolar mood disorders, differentiating between bipolar I and bipolar II.

5. Explain the similarities and differences between cyclothymia and bipolar disorder.

6. Describe the characteristics of rapid cycling depression/mania.

7. Explain how seasonal affective disorder may be related to environmental changes in sunlight.

8. Describe the symptoms and prevalence of mood disorder with postpartum onset.

9. Describe three principal patterns of attachment between children and their mothers and how these may be related to the development of later depression.

10. Discuss how attachment theory views the development of depression, explaining the concepts of anaclitic depression, introjective depression, and sociotropy.

11. Discuss how Beck's cognitive model views depression. What are three types of cognitive distortions that depressed individuals engage in?

12. Explain the hopelessness theory of depression.

13. Explain the rumination model of depression. What is meant by "a ruminative coping style"?

14. Discuss how interpersonal models, such as self-verification theory, explain depression.

15. Explain how life stress may be related to the development of depression.

16. Describe what family, adoption, and twin studies have shown concerning the heritability of depression.

17. Explain how neurotransmitter deficiencies are thought to lead to depression.

18. Explain how the endocrine system may be implicated in some instances of depression.

19. Describe the insights that neuroimaging studies have provided concerning hippocampal volume and depression.

20. Discuss what the findings of electrophysiological studies suggest concerning depression.

21. Describe how cognitive behaviour therapists treat depression.

22. Outline the three phases of treatment in interpersonal psychotherapy.

23. Identify three major classes of antidepressant medication, and explain the way that each increases available levels of neurotransmitters.

24. Discuss the benefits and shortcomings of lithium carbonate as a treatment for bipolar disorder.

25. Discuss how psychological and pharmacological treatments have been combined to treat mood disorders.

26. Discuss the benefits and shortcomings of electroconvulsive therapy for depression.

27. Explain the following terms:

    Suicidal ideation

    Suicidal gesture

    Parasuicide

    Suicide completers

28. Discuss the role of mental illness in suicide.

29. Discuss the following risk factors for suicide:

    Gender

    Age

    Culture/ethnicity

    Contagion

    Substance abuse disorders

Social factors

Psychological factors

Biological factors

30. Identify and discuss three factors used to assess suicide risk.

KEY WORDS

Mood disorder_____

_____

Major depressive disorder_____

_____

Anhedonia   _____

_____

Unipolar disorder   _____

_____

Bipolar disorder   _____

_____

Specifiers _____

_____

Stigma_____

_____

Dysthymic disorder _____

_____

Dysthymia_____

_____

Mania _____

_____

Bipolar I _____

_____

Bipolar II _____

_____

Hypomanic _____

_____

Cyclothymic disorder _____

_____

Cyclothymia _____

_____

With rapid cycling_____

_____

Seasonal affective disorder (SAD) _____

_____

Mood disorder with postpartum onset _____

_____

Secure attachment _____

_____

Anxious resistant attachment _____

_____

Anxious avoidant attachment _____

_____

Anaclitic depression _____

_____

Introjective depression _____

_____

Sociotropy _____

_____

Autonomous _____

_____

Schemata _____

_____

Cognitive triad _____

_____

Black-and-white thinking _____

_____

Overgeneralization _____

_____

Selective abstraction _____

_____

Hopelessness theory _____

_____

Rumination _____

_____

Ruminative coping style _____

_____

Self-verification theory _____

_____

Excessive reassurance seeking _____

_____

Diathesis-stress model _____

_____

Role transitions _____

_____

Adjustment disorder with depressed mood _____

_____

Social support _____

_____

Family studies _____

_____

Proband _____

_____

Adoption studies _____

_____

Concordant _____

_____

Linkage analysis _____

_____

Neurotransmitters _____

_____

Catecholamine _____

_____

Magnetic resonance imaging (MRI) _____

_____

Electroencephalograph (EEG) _____

_____

Frontal asymmetry _____

_____

Electroconvulsive therapy (ECT) _____

_____

Interpersonal psychotherapy (IPT) _____

_____

Tricyclics _____

Monoamine oxidase inhibitors (MAOIs) _____

Selective serotonin reuptake inhibitors (SSRIs) _____

Lithium carbonate _____

Suicide_____

Risk factors _____

FILL-IN-THE-BLANKS

1. Mood disorder diagnoses centre on two aspects: _____ and _____ of the symptoms.

2. For a diagnosis of major depressive disorder, a total of _____ symptoms must occur for at least _____ weeks.

3. _____ mood disorders are characterized by a one-way change in mood toward the negative direction, as opposed to _____ mood disorders, which include mood changes in both positive and negative directions.

4. _____ is characterized by a depressed mood that lasts for at least two years.

5. The disorder in which there are one or more manic episodes and usually one or more depressive episodes is referred to as bipolar _____ *(I or II).*

6. _____ episodes are similar to manic episodes but are not as extreme and do not involve psychotic features.

7. Although bipolar disorders themselves are equally distributed among men and women, _____ (*men/women*) make up 70 to 90 percent of those diagnosed with rapid cycling depression/mania.

8. _____ depression (also commonly known as *dependent depression*) is characterized by feelings of being unloved, unwanted, neglected, and abandoned.

9. _____ represents a personality type that is focused on positive interactions with others and is characterized by dependence on others for acceptance and approval.

10. _____ are interconnected beliefs, information, and examples used to organize and interpret information about the self and the world.

11. According to Beck, depressed patients often report a negative cognitive triad of thoughts about the _____, the _____, and the _____.

12. The pessimistic attributional style results in people making negative predictions by attributing negative events to causes that are _____ (the depressed person's own fault), _____ (likely to persist over time), and _____ (likely to affect many areas of life).

13. According to life stress models, role _____—such as transfer to a new school, getting married, having children, changing careers, or retiring—are common stressors that can affect one's vulnerability to depression.

14. The congruency hypothesis holds that depression will occur most frequently when the stressor is in the same category as a matching _____.

15. The evidence for a genetic contribution is _____ (*stronger/weaker*) for bipolar disorder than for unipolar depression.

16. The neurotransmitters _____ (a catecholamine) and _____ (an indoleamine) are thought to be involved in depression.

17. Typical frontal asymmetry in depression is reflected in _____ (*increased/decreased*) right-frontal activity and _____ (*increased/decreased*) left-frontal activity.

18. _____ is a cognitive error in which depressed people draw conclusions in the absence of data to support those conclusions.

19. Three major types of medications used to treat unipolar depression are _____, _____, and _____.

20. Lithium carbonate is the medication used most often to treat _____.

21. A _____ is the enactment of what appears to be a suicide attempt, but the method used or the severity of the behaviour is clearly not life threatening.

22. is an unsuccessful attempt at suicide, with the definite potential for death.

23. The study of those who have successfully committed suicide is referred to as a _____.

MULTIPLE CHOICE

1. Major depressive disorder

   a. occurs roughly twice as frequently in men as in women
   b. occurs roughly twice as frequently in women as in men
   c. occurs approximately equally frequently in the two sexes
   d. none of the above

2. The most frequent comorbid disorder with depression is

   a. anxiety
   b. suicide
   c. alcoholism
   d. anomie

3. _____ shows many of the same symptoms as major depression, except that those symptoms are less severe.

   a. bipolar affective disorder
   b. anomie
   c. cyclothymia
   d. dysthymia

4. Bipolar mood disorder

   a. occurs more frequently in males than in females
   b. occurs more frequently in females than in males
   c. is evenly distributed between males and females
   d. is so rare that no research has examined its relative incidence in males and females

5. Head injury, hyperthyroidism, antidepressant drug use, neurological conditions such as multiple sclerosis, and mental retardation are factors that have been linked to

   a. cyclothymia
   b. rapid cycling depression/mania
   c. depression with melancholic features
   d. anaclitic depression

6. The onset and offset of the symptoms of _____ are consistent with changes in weather, usually beginning in the fall or winter and ending in the spring.

    a. bipolar affective disorder
    b. cyclothymic disorder
    c. seasonal affective disorder
    d. dysthymic disorder

7. Clingy, anxious children who are uncertain of parent accessibility would likely be described as displaying _____ attachment.

    a. anxious avoidant
    b. anomic
    c. introjective
    d. anxious resistant

8. What type of thinking error or cognitive distortion, according to Beck's cognitive model of depression, can be seen most clearly in the following statement: "If I don't get an A in this course, I am a failure!"

    a. overgeneralization
    b. black-and-white thinking
    c. ruminative thinking
    d. hopeless thinking

9. Self-verification theory refers to

    a. the tendency for depressed individuals to focus continually and repeatedly on depressive symptoms, possible causes, and consequences
    b. the tendency for depressed individuals to expect negative outcomes concerning themselves, their world, and their future
    c. the tendency for depressed individuals to seek information from others that is consistent with their negative self-view
    d. the tendency for depressed individuals to "stir" in their negative moods

10. The diathesis-stress model views depression as resulting from

    a. the combination of vulnerability and life stress
    b. low levels of catecholamines in the brain, resulting in high levels of stress
    c. the tendency of individuals to view failure as being their own fault and due to personal characteristics that are stable parts of their personalities
    d. the stressful consequences of a negative view of the self, the world, and the future

11. Family studies indicate that relatives of people with bipolar disorder are _____ times more likely to develop bipolar disorder than individuals from the general population.

    a. 7 to 15
    b. 5 to 10
    c. 10 to 20
    d 20 to 30

12. Electrophysiological studies suggest a connection between depression and

    a. hippocampal atrophy
    b. catecholamine levels
    c. endocrine system functioning
    d. frontal EEG asymmetry

13. Which of the following treatment methods is best characterized as a brief and structured treatment that focuses on interpersonal disputes, role transitions, grief, and interpersonal deficits?

    a. interpersonal psychotherapy
    b. psychodynamic psychotherapy
    c. cognitive behaviour therapy
    d. sociotropic therapy

14. SSRIs increase available levels of neurotransmitters by

    a. inhibiting the reuptake of serotonin once it is released in the synapse
    b. inhibiting the release of substances that break down neurotransmitters
    c. enabling more neurotransmitters to be released into the synaptic cleft
    d. all of the above

15. Significant side effects of MAOIs include

    a. memory impairment
    b. the need for monitoring of patients' diets and restrictions of foods containing tyramine
    c. excessive urination and reduced kidney function
    d. blurred vision, constipation, dry mouth, and dizziness

16. Lithium carbonate is the traditionally accepted pharmacological treatment for

    a. seasonal affective disorder
    b. dysthymia
    c. anaclitic depression
    d. bipolar disorder

17. When ECT was first introduced as a treatment for depression, the most common patient complaints were

    a. memory impairment
    b. the need for close monitoring of diets and restrictions of foods containing tyramine
    c. excessive urination and reduced kidney function
    d. blurred vision, constipation, dry mouth, and dizziness

18. Although _____ are more likely to attempt suicide, _____ are more likely to be successful.

    a. men, women
    b. children, adults
    c. women, men
    d. adults, children

ANSWERS

FILL-IN-THE-BLANKS

1. severity; duration
2. five; two
3. unipolar; bipolar
4. dysthymic disorder
5. I
6. hypomanic
7. women
8. anaclitic
9. sociotropy
10. schemata
11. self; world; future
12. internal; stable; global
13. transitions
14. vulnerability
15. stronger
16. norepinephrine; serotonin
17. increased; decreased
18. arbitrary inference
19. tricyclics; MAOIs; and SSRIs
20. bipolar disorder
21. suicidal gesture
22. parasuicide
23. psychological autopsy

MULTIPLE CHOICE

1.	b	10.	a
2.	a	11.	a
3.	d	12.	d
4.	c	13.	a
5.	b	14.	a
6.	c	15.	b
7.	d	16.	d
8.	b	17.	a
9.	c	18.	c

CHAPTER 9

Schizophrenia

CHAPTER OUTLINE

LEARNING OBJECTIVES

When you have completed your study of the chapter, you should be able to:

1. Discuss whether schizophrenia existed in the distant past or is instead a recent illness.

2. Distinguish between the positive and negative symptoms of schizophrenia. Why are some symptoms referred to as positive whereas others are called negative?

3. Explain what hallucinations are, and indicate which is the most common modality of hallucination in schizophrenia.

4. Explain what delusions are, and describe each of the following five forms of delusions frequently seen in schizophrenia:

   Persecutory delusions

   Referential delusions

   Somatic delusions

   Religious delusions

   Delusions of grandeur

5. Describe how thought disorder reveals itself in the speech of schizophrenic patients.

6. Describe each of the following negative symptoms of schizophrenia:

   Avolition

   Alogia

   Affective flattening

7. Provide examples of what is meant by *grossly disorganized behaviour* in schizophrenia.

8. Identify and describe each of the five DSM-IV-TR diagnostic criteria for schizophrenia.

9. Which two Criterion-A DSM-IV-TR symptoms are weighted more heavily than others?

10. Describe the major characteristics of each of the following subtypes of schizophrenia:

    Paranoid

    Disorganized type

    Catatonic type

    Undifferentiated type

    Residual type

11. Explain how delusional disorder differs from schizophrenia.

12. Provide examples of each of the following three types of delusional disorder:

    Jealous type

    Somatic type

    Erotomanic type

13 Explain what is meant by the term *disease marker*. Discuss how digit span and eye movements may serve as markers for schizophrenia.

14. Describe the early views of the etiology of schizophrenia, specifically those held by Kraepelin, Bleuler, and Jung.

15. Discuss Meehl's diathesis-stress theory of schizophrenia. According to this theory, how is hypokrisia related to the development of schizophrenia?

16. Discuss how family studies suggest a familial genetic contribution to schizophrenia. What is the relevance of the notion of incomplete penetrance to the heritability of schizophrenia?

17. Discuss the possible roles of pregnancy and birth complications in the development of schizophrenia.

18. Describe the methods and findings of studies that attempt to identify early predictors in children of later schizophrenia in adulthood.

19. Describe the findings of research with schizophrenic patients using neuropsychological tests, such as the "F-A-S" technique and the Wisconsin Card Sorting Test. What are the limitations of these findings?

20. Identify two functional imaging techniques, and discuss their findings with regard to schizophrenic patients.

21. Discuss the controversy concerning the presence and role of brain abnormalities in schizophrenia.

22. Discuss the evidence suggesting the role of dopamine in schizophrenia. In what ways do stimulants, such as cocaine and amphetamine, lend support to the dopamine hypothesis?

23. Describe what researchers have found about the roles of dopamine levels and dopamine receptors in schizophrenia.

24. Explain how insulin coma and psychosurgery were used to treat schizophrenia.

25. Explain how promethazine was discovered as a treatment for schizophrenia.

26. What are the benefits and drawbacks of the use of antipsychotic medications in the treatment of schizophrenia?

27. Outline how cognitive-behaviour therapy has been used with patients with schizophrenia.

28. Explain how social skills training and stress management have been used with patients with schizophrenia.

KEY WORDS

Schizophrenia _____

_____

Auditory hallucinations _____

_____

Delusional thinking _____

_____

Positive symptoms _____

_____

Psychosis _____

_____

Delusions _____

_____

Hallucinations _____

_____

Thought and speech disorder _____

_____

Catatonic behaviour _____

_____

Negative symptoms _____

_____

Avolition _____

_____

Anhedonia_____

_____

Persecutory delusions _____

_____

Delusions of grandeur _____

_____

Loosening of associations _____

_____

Alogia _____

_____

Affective flattening _____

_____

Waxy flexibility _____

_____

Bizarre delusions _____

_____

Mood congruent _____

_____

Paranoid type _____

_____

Disorganized type _____

_____

Catatonic type _____

_____

Undifferentiated type _____

_____

Residual type _____

_____

Delusional disorder _____

_____

Jealous type _____

_____

Somatic type _____

_____

Erotomanic type _____

_____

Disease markers _____

_____

Sensitivity _____

_____

Specificity _____

_____

Digit span _____

_____

Cognitive marker _____

_____

Eye-tracking _____

_____

Schizophrenogenic mother _____

_____

Collective unconscious _____

_____

Social drift_____

_____

Diathesis-stress _____

_____

Hypokrisia_____

_____

Cognitive slippage _____

_____

Aversive drift _____

_____

Schizotype_____

_____

Familiality_____

_____

Penetrance _____

_____

Epigenetic _____

_____

Birth-related complications _____

_____

High-risk children _____

_____

Expressed emotion _____

_____

Cumulative liability _____

_____

Frontal lobe _____

_____

Neuropsychological tests _____

_____

Wisconsin Card Sorting Test _____

_____

Perseverate _____

_____

Frontal brain deficiency _____

_____

Meta-analysis _____

_____

Effect size _____

_____

Structural magnetic resonance imaging (MRI) _____

_____

Post-mortem examination _____

_____

Positron emission tomography (PET) _____

_____

Activation study _____

_____

Functional magnetic resonance imaging (fMRI) _____

_____

Left temporal lobe _____

_____

Amygdala _____

_____

Hippocampus _____

_____

Dopamine _____

_____

Neurotransmitters _____

_____

Receptors _____

_____

Ligands _____

_____

Dopamine-blocking drugs_____

_____

Insulin coma _____

_____

Psychosurgery_____

_____

Frontal lobotomy _____

_____

Chlorpromazine _____

_____

Risperidone _____

_____

Olanzapine _____

_____

Social stigma _____

_____

Cognitive-behaviour therapy _____

_____

Social skills training _____

_____

Stress management _____

_____

Family therapy _____

_____

Prevention of psychosis _____

_____

FILL-IN-THE-BLANKS

1. In North America and Europe, there is a _____% risk that a person will develop schizophrenia at some point in his or her life.

2. Although schizophrenia occurs throughout the world, it occurs most frequently in _____ socioeconomic groups.

3. Exaggerated, distorted adaptations of normal behaviour are referred to as _____ symptoms of schizophrenia.

4. _____, or apathy and loss of motivation, is a negative symptom of schizophrenia.

5. _____ are implausible beliefs, typically based on misinterpretation of experiences or perceptions.

6. _____ delusions involve the belief that common, inconsequential occurrences have significant and personal relevance.

7. Thought disorder reveals itself in the structure of spoken or written language, providing an objective index of schizophrenic disturbance. It is the _____ *(least/most)* common of the positive symptoms.

8. Disorganized schizophrenia tends to be the _____ *(least/most)* disabling of the symptom-based subtypes of schizophrenia.

9. The principle characteristic of _____ is a persisting but non-bizarre delusion that is not due to any other psychotic disorder.

10. Any objective psychological, as well as physical, sign of schizophrenia or of vulnerability to schizophrenia would be referred to as a _____ for the illness.

11. It was once thought that a severely rejecting mother could be _____, thereby creating the conditions for a weak and primitive ego in her children.

12. Meehl's theory proposes a biological diathesis, termed _____, that occurs throughout the brain, making nerve cells abnormally reactive to incoming stimulation.

13. In Meehl's theory, a person experiencing cognitive slippage and aversive drift is termed a _____.

14. Mechanisms that control or influence genes and their effects, referred to as _____ mechanisms, may be as important for the etiology of schizophrenia as the genes themselves.

15. The main disadvantage of the _____ method of assessing vulnerability to schizophrenia in children is the limited availability and variable accuracy of old records (and old memories).

16. Negative interpersonal communication, referred to as _____, directed at a family member with schizophrenia does not *cause* schizophrenia but can make it worse.

17. Neurological tests, such as the F-A-S technique and the Wisconsin Card Sorting Test, suggest, but do not prove, the role of _____ lobe impairment in schizophrenia.

18. Stimulants, such as cocaine and amphetamine, that accentuate or boost the activity of the neurotransmitter _____, can produce psychotic states.

19. _____ are chemicals that bind selectively with specific receptor sites.

20. _____ was the first genuine antipsychotic medication.

MULTIPLE CHOICE

1. Schizophrenia is characterized by both positive and negative symptoms. Positive symptoms

   a. are viewed as indicators of a potentially positive prognosis for the individual
   b. are exaggerated, distorted adaptations of normal behaviour
   c. refer to the absence or loss of typical behaviours or experiences
   d. all of the above

2. Beliefs that the individual has special powers or special knowledge are referred to as

   a. persecutory delusions
   c. referential delusions
   b. delusions of grandeur
   d. somatic delusions

3. Which are the most common form of hallucinations in schizophrenia?

   a. auditory
   c. olfactory
   b. visual
   d. tactile

4. Which is the least common of the positive symptoms of schizophrenia?

   a. hallucinations
   c. delusions
   b. thought disorder
   d. anhedonia

5. Which of the following is an example of a negative symptom of schizophrenia?

   a. catatonia
   b. avolition
   c. disorganized thought and speech
   d. delusions

6. Hallucinations that involve _____ are sufficient to satisfy Criterion A for a diagnosis of schizophrenia, even in the absence of any other Criterion-A characteristics.

   a. the perception of several voices having a discussion

   b. odd odours

   c. bizarre tactile experiences, such as the feeling that one's skin is covered with insects

   d. peculiar visual experiences, such as seeing spirits or ghosts

7. The disorganized type of schizophrenia

   a. is associated with later onset and is thought to have a better prognosis than the other subtypes

   b. is associated with good prognosis in patients with no delusions but poor prognosis in those who experience delusions

   c. is associated with good prognosis if treated early with electroconvulsive therapy

   d. is typically associated with early onset and is thought to have the poorest prognosis

8. The most common subtype of schizophrenia is the

   a. undifferentiated subtype

   b. residual subtype

   c. paranoid subtype

   d. none of the above

9. The _____ subtype of schizophrenia is defined by acute psychomotor disturbance, which may present as immobility (including cataplexy or stupor) and extreme negativism and rigidity.

   a. paranoid

   b. disorganized

   c. catatonic

   d. undifferentiated

10. Swiss psychiatrist Carl Jung told of a patient's delusion that was strikingly parallel to a belief held in the ancient Persian religion of Mithraism. Jung felt that this patient's belief illustrated the connection between psychosis and

   a. social stigma

   b. a weak and primitive ego

   c. expressed emotion

   d. the collective unconscious

11. Which of the following explanations of the relation between social class and schizophrenia may be true?

   a. Schizophrenia occurs much more frequently among people from middle to higher socioeconomic classes than in those from lower socioeconomic classes.

b. The stress of being a member of the middle to higher socioeconomic classes may be a factor in the development of schizophrenia.

c. There is no clear relation between socioeconomic status and schizophrenia.

d. It may be that people who have schizophrenia drift to a lower socioeconomic status as a result of their symptoms.

12. According to Paul Meehl, hypokrisia does not cause mental retardation or other gross disorders of brain function. What it produces instead is a more subtle disturbance, which Meehl called

a. cognitive slippage
b. aversive drift
c. penetrance
d. cumulative liability

13. There is recent evidence suggesting that fetal exposure to the _____ virus during the fifth month of pregnancy may be associated with an increased risk of schizophrenia later in life.

a. flu
b. HIV
c. mumps
d. rubella

14. The performance of schizophrenic patients on neuropsychological tests, such as the "F-A-S" technique and the Wisconsin Card Sorting Test, suggests that _____ deficiency may be implicated in schizophrenia.

a. temporal lobe
b. hippocampus
c. amygdala
d. frontal lobe

15. The finding that expressed emotion occurs not only in the families of people with schizophrenia but also in families of those with mood and eating disorders suggests that

a. negative family attitudes may make it difficult to adjust to psychological problems in general
b. schizophrenia is likely related to mood and eating disorders
c. schizophrenia, mood disorders, and eating disorders all seem to share the same cause
d. family attitudes tell us nothing about the development of schizophrenia

16. Approximately _____ % of people who have a schizophrenic parent develop the disorder themselves.

    a. 1
    b. 8
    c. 13
    d. 19

17. Children at risk for schizophrenia

    a. have a high incidence of viral infections
    b. may be withdrawn and socially reclusive or antisocial and aggressive
    c. are frequently categorized as gifted by their teachers
    d. rarely have any relatives diagnosed with the illness

18. Which of the following does *not* appear to be evidence for the role of dopamine in schizophrenia?

    a. Antipsychotic medications, such as chlorpromazine, reduce symptoms by blocking dopamine receptors.
    b. Dopamine levels in the brain and cerebral spinal fluid are elevated in people with schizophrenia.
    c. Drugs, such as cocaine and amphetamine, can produce psychotic reactions that resemble acute schizophrenic episodes.
    d. All of the above are true.

19. Chlorpromazine and other antipsychotic medications are most effective in alleviating

    a. social disabilities
    b. social stigma
    c. hallucinations, delusions, and thought disorder
    d. avolition, alogia, and affective flattening

20. Recent Canadian evidence suggests that the greatest therapeutic effect of cognitive behaviour therapy with schizophrenic patients may be in reducing

    a. agitation, mania, and mood disturbances
    b. hallucinations, delusions, and thought disorder
    c. negative symptoms of schizophrenia
    d. drug-induced psychotic episodes

ANSWERS

FILL-IN-THE-BLANKS

1. 1
2. lower
3. positive
4. avolition
5. delusions
6. referential
7. least
8. most
9. delusional disorder
10. disease marker
11. schizophrenogenic
12. hypokrisia
13. schizotype
14. epigenetic
15. follow-back
16. expressed emotion
17. frontal
18. dopamine
19. ligands
20. chlorpromazine

MULTIPLE CHOICE

1.	b	11.	d
2.	b	12.	a
3.	a	13.	a
4.	b	14.	d
5.	b	15.	a
6.	a	16.	c
7.	d	17.	b
8.	c	18.	b
9.	c	19.	c
10.	d	20.	c

CHAPTER 10

Eating Disorders

CHAPTER OUTLINE

LEARNING OBJECTIVES

When you have completed your study of the chapter, you should be able to:

1. Describe the typical characteristics of anorexia nervosa.

2. Differentiate between objective and subjective binge eating.

3. Describe the typical characteristics of bulimia nervosa.

4. Explain the similarities and the differences between anorexia nervosa and bulimia nervosa.

5. Discuss the incidence and prevalence of eating disorders. Has this changed over time?

6. Outline the four DSM-IV-TR diagnostic criteria for a diagnosis of anorexia nervosa.

7. Identify and describe the two DSM-IV-TR subtypes of anorexia nervosa.

8. Outline the DSM-IV-TR diagnostic criteria for a diagnosis of bulimia nervosa.

9. Identify and describe the two DSM-IV-TR subtypes of bulimia nervosa.

10. Outline the DSM-IV-TR criteria for the diagnosis of Eating Disorder Not Otherwise Specified (EDNOS).

11. Outline the DSM-IV-TR criteria for binge-eating disorder.

12. Differentiate between bulimia nervosa and the binge-eating/purging type of anorexia.

13. Differentiate between the nonpurging type of bulimia and binge-eating disorder.

14. Explain how some researchers conceptualize eating disorders on a spectrum rather than as separate diagnostic categories.

15. Describe the procedures typically used in the assessment of eating disorders.

16. Describe the physical and psychological consequences of eating disorders.

17. Discuss how serotonin may play a role in anorexia and bulimia. What does genetic research offer here?

18. Explain how sociocultural pressure can lead to body dissatisfaction and may result in an eating disorder. What differences are seen between males and females in this phenomenon?

19. Discuss how family factors may contribute to the development of eating disorders.

20. Discuss how personality factors may be related to eating disorders. Why it is difficult to draw firm conclusions about the relationship between personality and eating disorders?

21. Explain the relationship between low self-esteem and eating disorders. Comment on the problem interpreting the direction of this relationship.

22. Explain how physical changes associated with puberty may be important in the development of eating disorders. How do these differ for females and males?

23. Discuss what is known concerning the association between sexual abuse and eating disorders.

24. Describe how predisposing factors, precipitating factors, and perpetuating factors may interact in the development of bulimia nervosa.

25. Discuss what is known about eating disorders in males.

26. Discuss the effectiveness of antidepressant medication in the treatment of bulimia and anorexia.

27. Outline three stages of cognitive-behaviour therapy treatment for bulimia. How effective is cognitive-behaviour therapy in the treatment of bulimia and anorexia?

28. Explain how interpersonal therapy has been used in the treatment of bulimia nervosa.

29. Discuss how family therapy has been used in the treatment of anorexia.

30. Describe the effectiveness of self-help methods in the treatment of bulimia.

31. Discuss the effectiveness of programs designed to prevent eating disorders.

KEY WORDS

Purging _____

_____

Objective binge _____

_____

Anorexia nervosa _____

_____

Amenorrhea _____

_____

Restricting type _____

_____

Binge-eating/purging type _____

_____

Bulimia nervosa _____

_____

Purging type _____

_____

Nonpurging type _____

_____

BMI _____

_____

Eating Disorder Examination (EDE) _____

_____

Lanugo _____

_____

Russell's sign _____

_____

Precipitating factors _____

_____

Perpetuating factors _____

_____

FILL-IN-THE-BLANKS

1. _____ nervosa is characterized by the pursuit of thinness to dangerously low weight levels, while _____ nervosa is characterized by a binge/purge syndrome in people who are generally in the normal weight range.

2. Individuals with anorexia have an intense fear of _____. This fear is paradoxical, given that they are in fact _____.

3. An _____ binge consists of eating a large amount of food in a specified time period. In contrast, a _____ binge involves reported binge eating, although only small or normal amounts of food have been eaten during the episode.

4. Mortality rates for individuals with eating disorders are estimated to be approximately _____ percent.

5. DSM-IV-TR subtypes anorexia nervosa into a _____ type and a _____ type.

6. DSM-IV-TR subtypes bulimia nervosa into a _____ type and a _____ type.

7. _____, defined as "the absence of three conceptual menstrual cycles," is a DSM-IV-TR criterion for a diagnosis of anorexia nervosa.

8. _____ type anorexics attain their extremely low body weights through strict dieting and sometimes excessive exercise.

9. Some researchers have proposed that eating disorders be conceptualized on a _____ rather than as separate diagnostic categories.

10. According to Fairburn and his colleagues, in mid-adolescence, eating disorders most typically resemble _____, whereas the eating disorders of late adolescence and early adulthood tend to resemble _____.

11. Many researchers and even clinicians use a structured interview called the _____ to aid their assessments of eating disorders.

12. In individuals with anorexia, a fine downy hair called _____ may grow on the body to maintain body warmth.

13. Individuals who self-induce vomiting may exhibit scrapes or calluses on the backs of their hands or knuckles, referred to as _____.

14. It appears that _____ is associated with an underactive serotonin system while _____ is associated with reduced tryptophan availability and decreased serotonin synthesis.

15. The main features of eating disorders _____ (are/are not) different in males than in females.

16. Among _____ (males/females), homosexuals may be at greater risk for eating disorders.

17. Numerous studies have indicated that the majority of males who are dissatisfied with their weight would like to _____ their current weight.

18. Attempts to treat _____ with pharmacological agents have not been successful.

19. One of the few therapies that have been found effective in the treatment of anorexia nervosa in controlled trials is _____.

MULTIPLE CHOICE

1. A review of outcome studies shows that the _____ subtype of anorexia has a poorer long-term prognosis than the _____ subtype.

    a. binge eating/purging; restricting   b. bulimic; nonpurging
    c. nonpurging; bulimic   d. restricting; binge eating/purging

2. Rather than recognizing their dangerously low weight as a problem, people with anorexia

   a. are frequently unconcerned about weight
   b. frequently gain excessive weight, which they view as a problem
   c. have an intense fear of gaining weight
   d. cycle between being extremely underweight and excessively overweight

3. Unlike anorexia nervosa, people with bulimia nervosa

   a. tend not to be concerned about their weight
   b. are generally at least 15% overweight
   c. always use purging as a way of preventing weight gain
   d. are generally in the normal weight range

4. One of the DSM-IV-TR diagnostic criteria for anorexia involves a distortion in the experience and significance of body weight. Such distortions may include

   a. perception of oneself as weighing more than one does or being larger than one is
   b. denial of the seriousness of one's current lowered weight
   c. determination of self-worth based primarily on body weight
   d. all of the above

5. Recent reports estimate that for every male diagnosed with anorexia or bulimia, there are _____ females with these disorders.

   a. 3–5   b. 10–15
   c. 15–20   d. 20–25

6. Many individuals with anorexia

   a. seldom exercise because they are so physically weak
   b. exercise only when necessary
   c. exercise excessively as a way of burning calories
   d. would prefer to purge rather than exercise, if given the choice

7. How does binge-eating disorder differ from bulimia?

   a Individuals with binge-eating disorder engage in recurrent episodes of bingeing, which is almost always followed by excessive exercise.
   b. Individuals with binge-eating disorder engage in recurrent episodes of bingeing, which is almost always followed by purging.
   c. Individuals with binge-eating disorder engage in recurrent episodes of bingeing but do not engage in inappropriate compensatory behaviours.
   d. Individuals with binge-eating disorder engage in recurrent episodes of bingeing but seem not to be aware or concerned about their excessive eating.

8. Fairburn and associates have pointed out that eating disorder diagnoses tend to change in a systematic way over the lifespan. In _____, eating disorders most typically resemble anorexia nervosa.

    a. adulthood   b. childhood
    c. late adolescence   d. mid-adolescence

9. Many researchers and even clinicians use a semi-structured interview known as the _____ to assess eating disorders.

    a. Eating Disorder Examination (EDE)
    b. Anorexia/Bulimia Intake Interview (ABII)
    c. Interview for the Assessment of Eating Disorders (IAED)
    d. Diagnostic Interview for the Assessment of Eating Disorders (DIAED)

10. In research conducted with World War II conscientious objectors who were subjected to a state of semi-starvation, which of the following was associated with extreme weight loss?

    a. increased sex drive   b. decreased focus on food
    c. increases in emotional stability   d. decreases in heart rate

11. Research has indicated that serotonin may be associated in the pathophysiology of eating disorders. Specifically, bulimia is associated with

    a. an underactive serotonin system
    b. reduced tryptophan availability and decreased serotonin synthesis
    c. excess serotonin availability
    d. an overactive serotonin system

12. Twin, family, and molecular genetic studies suggest that _____ of the variance in eating disorders can be accounted for by genetic factors.

    a. less than 10%   b. over 50%
    c. 20–25 %   d. between 30% and 40%

13. According to the Women's Health Surveillance Report

    a. the prevalence of obesity among women has increased from 18% to 25% from 1985 to 2000/2001
    b. the prevalence of obesity among women has actually declined from 1985 to 2000/2001
    c. the prevalence of overweight among women has increased from 19% to 26% from 1985 to 2000/2001
    d. although the prevalence of overweight among women has increased from 1985 to 2000/2001, the prevalence of obesity has remained stable across the same period

14. Mothers who have an eating disorder

    a. feed their children on a very regular schedule and seldom use food with their children for non-nutritive purposes
    b. do not feed their children as regularly as nondisordered mothers but are much less likely to use food for non-nutritive purposes with their children
    c. do not feed their children as regularly as nondisordered mothers and are more likely to use food for non-nutritive purposes with their children
    d. feed their children on a very regular schedule but frequently use food for non-nutritive purposes with their children

15. Which of the following groups displays the highest rates of comorbid substance abuse?

    a. individuals who binge eat
    b. people with anorexia who use excessive exercise as their primary means of weight control
    c. restricting anorexics
    d. none of the above

16. Garner and Garfinkel (1980) propose that bulimia nervosa develops because of an interaction between predisposing, precipitating, and perpetuating factors. Which of the following would be considered a precipitating factor?

    a. reduced basal metabolism rate   b. dieting
    c. social isolation   d. being underweight

17. When university students who were restrained eaters were led to believe that they had gained five pounds in an experiment,

    a. they proceeded to report feeling bad about themselves and excessively restrained their eating when food was made available
    b. they proceeded to report feeling bad about themselves and to overeat when food was made available
    c. they were uninfluenced by this false information and continued to eat at pre-experiment levels when food was made available
    d. although they were uninfluenced by this false information, they showed restraint in their eating when food was made available

18. Research indicates the effectiveness of which of the following treatments for bulimia nervosa?

    a. antidepressant medication
    b. cognitive-behavioural therapy
    c. interpersonal therapy
    d. all of the above

ANSWERS

FILL-IN-THE-BLANKS

1. anorexia; bulimia
2. gaining weight; underweight
3. objective; subjective
4. 5 to 8
5. restricting; binge eating/purging
6. purging; nonpurging
7. amenorrhea
8. restricting
9. spectrum
10. anorexia nervosa; bulimia nervosa
11. Eating Disorder Examination
12. lanuga
13. Russell's sign
14. bulimia; anorexia
15. are not
16. males
17. increase
18. anorexia nervosa
19. family therapy

MULTIPLE CHOICE

1.	a	10.	d
2.	c	11.	a
3.	d	12.	b
4.	d	13.	c
5.	b	14.	c
6.	c	15.	a
7.	c	16.	b
8.	d	17.	b
9.	a	18.	d

CHAPTER 11

Substance-Related Disorders

CHAPTER OUTLINE

HISTORICAL PERSPECTIVE

DIAGNOSIS AND ASSESSMENT

Defining Substance-Related Concepts

Polysubstance Abuse

ALCOHOL

History of Use

Canadian Consumption Patterns

Effects

Etiology

Treatment

BARBITURATES AND BENZODIAZEPINES

Prevalence

Effects

Dependency

Treatment

STIMULANTS

Tobacco

LEARNING OBJECTIVES

1. Compare the DSM-IV diagnostic criteria for substance abuse and substance dependence.

2. Describe the characteristics of both physiological and psychological dependence.

3. Discuss the health and treatment concerns associated with polysubstance abuse.

4. Identify and describe the four categories of drinkers.

5. Discuss the short-term and long-term effects of alcohol abuse. Describe the problems associated with alcoholism.

6. Describe the characteristics of fetal alcohol syndrome.

7. Discuss the roles of each of the following in the development of alcoholism:

   Genetic factors

   Neurobiological influences

   Psychological factors

   Sociocultural factors

8. Describe the Minnesota model treatment plan for alcohol dependence.

9. Discuss the role of medication in the treatment of alcoholism.

10. Describe the origins of Alcoholics Anonymous. Identify and describe the goals and the steps involved in its therapy program.

11. Explain the importance of relapse prevention in the treatment of alcoholism.

12. Identify the importance of marital and family therapy programs. Describe the goal of treatment.

13. Discuss the results and effects of Mark and Linda Sobell's controversial study on controlled drinking.

14. Discuss the short-term and long-term effects of cigarette smoking, including the effects of second-hand smoke and potential health risks of smoking during pregnancy.

15. Outline which drugs fit into the category of depressants. Discuss their effects and treatment for their abuse.

16. Describe the effects of nicotine.

17. Describe the psychological and biological treatments for smoking.

18. Describe the original purpose for amphetamines and the prevalence of amphetamine use in Canada.

19. Discuss the effects of chronic use of stimulants.

20. Describe the short-term and long-term effects of cocaine.

21. Explain the psychological and biological treatments used for amphetamine and cocaine abuse.

22. Describe the effects of caffeine, explaining how they are dose-related.

23. Describe the effects of opioids, and discuss the treatment for opioid abuse.

24. Explain how harm reduction approaches differ from treatment approaches.

25. Describe the perceptual, physical, and motivational effects of cannabis use.

26. Discuss the present debate concerning the medical use of marijuana for certain disorders.

27. Describe the effects of hallucinogens, and discuss the issue of dependency concerning these substances.

28 Identify and discuss the similarities and differences between substance abuse and gambling.

KEY WORDS

Substance intoxication _____

_____

Substance abuse _____

_____

Substance dependence _____

_____

Physiological dependence_____

_____

Tolerance _____

_____

Withdrawal _____

_____

Psychological dependence _____

_____

Habituation _____

_____

Impairment of control _____

_____

Polysubstance abuse _____

_____

Synergistic _____

_____

Low-risk drinking guidelines _____

_____

Ethyl alcohol _____

_____

Blood alcohol level (BAL) _____

_____

Alcohol dehydrogenase _____

_____

Blackouts _____

_____

Korsakoff's psychosis _____

_____

Fetal alcohol syndrome (FAS) _____

_____

Behavioural disinhibition _____

_____

Negative emotionality _____

_____

Tension reduction _____

_____

Alcohol expectancy theory _____

_____

Behavioural tolerance _____

_____

Minnesota model _____

_____

Antagonist drug _____

_____

Agonist drug _____

_____

Antabuse _____

_____

Relapse _____

_____

Brief intervention _____

_____

Depressants _____

_____

Abstinence syndrome _____

_____

Stimulants _____

_____

Nicotine _____

_____

Amphetamines _____

_____

Toxic psychosis _____

_____

Opioids _____

_____

Endogenous opiates _____

_____

Exogenous opiates _____

_____

Harm reduction approaches _____

_____

Methadone_____

_____

Cannabis _____

_____

THC _____

_____

Amotivational syndrome _____

_____

Hallucinogens _____

_____

Flashback _____

_____

FILL-IN-THE-BLANKS

1. The first alcoholic beverage that humans consumed was _____.

2. _____ refers to the simultaneous misuse of multiple substances, which may cause physical dangers because they are often _____.

3. The effective chemical found in alcoholic beverages that reduces anxiety and creates a sense of well being is _____.

4. According to low-risk drinking guidelines, daily alcohol intake should not exceed _____ drinks, and weekly intake should not exceed _____ drinks for men and _____ drinks for women.

5. Maternal alcohol consumption can cause _____ syndrome.

6. Alcohol is broken down in the liver into a by-product called _____.

7. _____ is a neurotransmitter suggested in the development of alcoholism.

8. _____ is a medication that targets the neurotransmitters that mediate alcohol's effect on the brain, blocking its pleasurable effects.

9. The main goal of Alcoholics Anonymous is _____.

10. _____ is a treatment model that emphasizes the identification of potential high-risk situations and the development of strategies to deal with them.

11. _____ are drugs that inhibit neurotransmitter activity in the central nervous system.

12. _____ are drugs that have an arousing effect on the central nervous system.

13. Nicotine belongs to the class of drugs referred to as _____.

14. Biological treatments for smoking work on the principle of _____.

15. Amphetamines have effects on the body similar to those of the naturally occurring hormone_____.

16. Repeated high doses of amphetamine can cause hallucinations, delirium, and paranoia, a condition known as_____.

17. _____ involves heating and smoking the residue of cocaine.

18. Mixing heroin with water and injecting it to produce an intense high is called _____.

19. The psychoactive effects of cannabis are caused primarily by the chemical _____.

20. Experiencing a transference of sensory experiences between modalities, such as "hearing" colours or "feeling" sounds, is called _____.

MULTIPLE CHOICE

1. Requiring increasing amounts of a substance to achieve effects that used to occur with smaller amounts is called

    a. withdrawal
    c. habituation

    b. tolerance
    d. synergism

2. Women are more likely to become intoxicated because they have lower levels of

    a. tolerance
    c. alcohol dehydrogenase

    b. body fat
    d. citrated calcium carbamate

3. Alcohol can effect eye- and hand coordination at BALs as low as

    a. 01
    c. 05

    b. 03
    d. 08

4. It has been a popular belief that long-term alcohol abuse may cause permanent cell loss in brain areas associated with _____; however, research is conflicting, with some evidence of axon regrowth following an extended period of abstinence.

    a. Korsakoff's psychosis
    c. Parkinson's disease

    b. Tourette's syndrome
    d. Multiple sclerosis

5. Most health care providers recommend that during pregnancy women should

    a. consume no more than 1 drink per day
    b. maintain abstinence
    c. consume no more than 9 drinks per week
    d. practise controlled drinking

6. Neurobiological research suggests that sons of alcoholic fathers have higher than normal rates of

    a. P300 amplitudes   b. alpha waves
    c. fast beta waves   d. none of the above

7. The procedure for treatment emphasized by the Minnesota model involves all of the following, *except*

    a. detoxification   b. education
    c. individual counselling   d. aversion therapy

8. During treatment for barbiturate abuse, patients may experience _____, characterized by insomnia, headaches, aching all over the body, anxiety, and depression.

    a. toxic psychosis
    b. amotivational syndrome
    c. abstinence syndrome
    d. chronic fatigue

9. Psychological treatment for smoking focuses on all of the following, *except*

    a. self-monitoring   b. goal-setting
    c. problem solving   d. reinforcement

10. Stimulants influence the rate of uptake of the neurotransmitter

    a. dopamine
    b. norepinephrine
    c. serotonin
    d. all of the above

11. Continuous use of cocaine may result in

    a. mood swings
    b. loss of interest in sex
    c. weight loss
    d. all of the above

12. Approximately _____ of Canadians are described as physically dependent upon caffeine.

    a. 10%   b. 20%
    c. 30%   d. 40%

13. The body's natural painkillers are known as

    a. endogenous opiates
    b. exogenous opiates
    c. benzodiazepines
    d. monoamine oxidase

14. Which medication is typically used in the treatment of opioid abuse?

    a. methadone
    b. benzodiazepines
    c. bromocriptine
    d. disulfiram

15. A potential result of long-term cannabis abuse is

    a. hallucinations
    b. abstinence syndrome
    c. irregular heart rate
    d. amotivational syndrome

16. Few withdrawal effects have been associated with the abstinence of

    a. cannabis
    b. hallucinogens
    c. opioids
    d. cocaine

17. Methylated amphetamines, such as Ecstasy, are known for their

    a. stimulant and hallucinogenic properties
    b. ability to suppress the sex drive
    c. tendency to increase aggressive impulses
    d. tendency to cause paranoid delusions

18. Animal studies suggest that moderate or greater use of Ecstasy may lead to a permanent depletion of

    a. dopamine   b. norepinephrine
    c. serotonin   d. adrenaline

ANSWERS

FILL-IN-THE-BLANKS

1. mead
2. polysubstance abuse; synergistic
3. ethyl alcohol
4. 2; 14; 9
5. Fetal alcohol
6. acetaldehyde
7. GABA
8. Naltrexone (an antagonist drug)
9. abstinence
10. relapse prevention
11. depressants
12. stimulants
13. stimulants
14. nicotine replacement
15. adrenaline
16. toxic psychosis
17. freebasing
18. mainlining
19. *delta-9-tetrahydrocannabinol* (THC)
20. synesthesia

MULTIPLE CHOICE

1.	b	10.	d
2.	c	11.	d
3.	a	12.	b
4.	a	13.	a
5.	b	14.	a
6.	c	15.	d
7.	d	16.	b
8.	c	17.	a
9.	c	18.	c

CHAPTER 12

The Personality Disorders

CHAPTER OUTLINE

CLUSTER B: DRAMATIC, EMOTIONAL, OR ERRATIC DISORDERS

Antisocial Personality Disorder and Psychopathy: A Confusion of Diagnoses

Borderline Personality Disorder

Histrionic Personality Disorder

Narcissistic Personality Disorder

CLUSTER C: ANXIOUS AND FEARFUL DISORDERS

Avoidant Personality Disorder

Dependent Personality Disorder

Obsessive-Compulsive Personality Disorder

TREATMENT

Object-Relations Therapy

Cognitive-Behavioural Approaches

Pharmacological Interventions

LEARNING OBJECTIVES

When you have completed your study of the chapter, you should be able to:

1. Discuss the relationship between personality traits and personality disorders.

2. Identify three broad clusters of personality disorders

3. Describe five formal criteria provided by DSM-IV-TR for defining personality disorders.

4. Discuss how gender and cultural issues can influence the reliability of diagnosis of personality disorders.

5. Explain the difference between comorbidity and diagnostic overlap, and discuss the relevance of these issues to the diagnosis of disorders.

6. Explain the psychodynamic view of the development of personality disorder.

7. Describe how attachment theory accounts for the development of personality disorder.

8. Discuss the cognitive-behavioural explanations of the development of personality disorders.

9. Describe the biological explanations suggested for certain personality disorders.

10. Describe the major characteristics of paranoid personality disorder.

11. Describe the major characteristics of schizoid personality disorder.

12. Describe the major characteristics of schizotypal personality disorder.

13. Describe the major characteristics of antisocial personality disorder.

14. Discuss the differences between DSM-IV-TR diagnostic criteria for antisocial personality disorder and earlier diagnoses of psychopathy or sociopathy.

15. Discuss how both family environment and biological factors may contribute to the development of APD.

16. Explain the fearlessness hypothesis in APD.

17. Discuss the difficulties faced by clinicians attempting to treat APD.

18. Describe the major characteristics of psychopathy.

19. Discuss the hypothesized roles of brain abnormalities and neurotransmitters in the etiology of psychopathy.

20. Distinguish between fundamental psychopathy and secondary psychopathy.

21. Describe the major characteristics of borderline personality disorder.

22. Discuss the role of family factors, including insecure attachment, in the development of borderline personality disorder.

23. Describe the major characteristics of histrionic personality disorder.

24. Describe the major characteristics of narcissistic personality disorder.

25. Describe the major characteristics of avoidant personality disorder.

26. Describe the major characteristics of dependent personality disorder.

27. Describe the major characteristics of obsessive-compulsive personality disorder.

28. Discuss how object-relations theory and cognitive-behavioural approaches (including dialectical behaviour therapy) attempt to treat personality disorders.

29. Discuss the effectiveness of pharmacological interventions in treating personality disorders.

KEY WORDS

Traits _____

_____

Personality disorders _____

_____

Clusters _____

_____

Prevalence _____

_____

Egosyntonic _____

_____

Comorbidity _____

_____

Overlap _____

_____

Attachment theory_____

_____

Suspiciousness _____

_____

Delusion _____

_____

Emotional responsiveness_____

_____

Eccentricity _____

_____

Psychopaths _____

_____

Sociopaths_____

_____

Polythetic _____

_____

Fearlessness hypothesis _____

_____

Oppositional behaviour _____

_____

Responsivity factor _____

_____

Instability _____

_____

Anxious ambivalent _____

_____

Cognitive restructuring _____

_____

Dialectical behaviour therapy _____

_____

FILL-IN-THE-BLANKS

1. According to DSM-IV-TR, it is only when personality traits are _____ and _____ that they constitute a personality disorder.

2. The terms *overlap* and *comorbidity* are often used synonymously in the literature but in fact refer to two conceptually distinct features of diagnosis. Whereas _____ describes the co-occurrence in the same person of two or more different disorders, _____ refers to the similarity of symptoms in two or more different disorders.

3. Psychoanalysts see personality disorder as resulting from disturbances in the _____ relationship.

4. _____ theory proposes that children learn how to relate to others, particularly in affectionate ways, by the way in which their parents relate to them.

5. Pervasive suspiciousness regarding the motives of other people and a tendency to interpret what others say and do as personally meaningful in a negative way are the primary features of patients diagnosed as having _____ personality disorder.

6. Individuals with _____ personality disorder seem determined to avoid intimate involvement with others and display little emotional responsiveness.

7. "A pervasive pattern of disregard for, and violation of, the rights of others that begins in childhood or early adolescence and continues into adulthood" (*APA*, 1994, p. 645) is the essential defining feature of _____ personality disorder.

8. Individuals with a persistent pattern of antisocial behaviour have been referred to as _____, sociopaths, or dyssocial personalities.

9. The remittance over time of antisocial behaviours in APD individuals has been described as the _____ factor.

10. Fluctuations in mood, an unstable sense of identity, and instability in relationships characterize _____ personality disorder.

11. Individuals who strongly desire intimacy with others and who consequently persistently seek out romantic partners, yet who back away from relationships when they begin to get close to their partner, display an interpersonal attachment style described as _____.

12. _____ personality disorder is characterized by attention-seeking behaviours and flamboyance and the tendency to be overly dramatic in emotional displays and over-responsive to events that others would consider insignificant.

13. _____ personality disorder is characterized by a pervasive pattern of avoiding interpersonal contacts and an extreme sensitivity to criticism and disapproval.

14. Fear of relying on oneself and of making decisions characterize _____ personality disorder.

15. Inflexibility and a desire for perfection characterize _____ personality disorder.

MULTIPLE CHOICE

1. Which of the following is *not* one of the broad clusters into which DSM-IV-TR organizes personality disorders?

    a. odd and eccentric disorders
    b. dramatic, emotional, or erratic disorders
    c. anxious and fearful disorders
    d. dangerous and violent disorders

2. The functioning of many individuals with personality disorders is _____; that is, they do not view their behaviour as problematic.

    a. egosyntonic   b. egodystonic
    c. nonchalant   d. disinterested

3. Psychoanalysts see personality disorder as resulting from disturbances in

   a. adult attachment relationships
   b. core belief systems
   c. separation-individuation
   d. parents' interpersonal styles

4. Attachment theory argues that poor attachments lead to

   a. deficits in developing intimacy
   b. difficulty in separation-individuation
   c. rigid and inflexible schemas
   d. all of the above

5. According to cognitive-behavioural perspectives, personality-disordered individuals display

   a. rigid and inflexible schemas
   b. difficulty in separation-individuation
   c. deficits in developing intimacy
   d. all of the above

6. Suspiciousness, difficulties dealing with ambiguity, and the tendency to misread social cues as evidence of hostility by others are characteristic of

   a. schizoid personality disorder
   b. avoidant personality disorder
   c. paranoid personality disorder
   d. borderline personality disorder

7. Many people with _____ personality disorder are eccentric in thought and behaviour, and are extremely superstitious.

   a. schizoid
   b. schizotypal
   c. dependent
   d. paranoid

8. Which of the following are characteristics of antisocial personality disorder?

   a. callousness, deceitfulness, irresponsibility, impulsivity, and recklessness
   b. suspiciousness, jealousy, preoccupied with power and control, and isolation
   c. eccentricity of thought and behaviour, social isolation, and superstitiousness
   d. fluctuations in mood, an unstable sense of identity, impulsivity, unpredictability, and instability in relationships

9. The fearlessness hypothesis

    a. explains the suspiciousness of paranoids as a means of reducing fear and uncertainty in their lives
    b. explains the social isolation of avoidant individuals in terms of reducing their fear of criticism
    c. explains the instability in relationships characteristic of borderlines as a means of reducing fear of possible rejection
    d. claims that psychopaths have a higher threshold for feeling fear than do others

10. Schmauk's research on the effects of punishment in psychopaths indicated that

    a. psychopaths are unresponsive to punishment
    b. psychopaths often "burn out" when exposed to high levels of punishment that extend over a long period of time
    c. psychopaths are differentially responsive to different kinds of punishment
    d. severe physical punishment is the only effective punishment for psychopaths

11. Porter (1996) has suggested that there are two pathways that can lead to the development of psychopathy. In the case of secondary psychopathy, the disorder is the result of

    a. a biological predisposition that hinders the development of affective bonds
    b. negative emotional experiences early in childhood
    c. the development of rigid schemas pertaining to one's past, present, and future
    d. a high threshold for feeling fear

12. The interpersonal attachment style of borderlines can be described as

    a. secure
    b. anxious avoidant
    c. anxious ambivalent
    d. anxious inhibited

13. Borderline individuals

    a. actively avoid social interactions, tending to restrict social interactions only to those they trust not to denigrate them
    b. seem unable to tolerate being alone and accordingly become desperate about their relationships, alternating between idealizing and devaluing their partners
    c. tend not to enjoy relationships of any type, apparently preferring to be alone
    d. not only allow, but seem to desperately need others to assume responsibility for important aspects of their lives

14. George has been in trouble with the authorities most of his life. At school, punishments like detentions and suspensions only seemed to make things worse. As an adult, he's been unable to hold down a job because he can't be trusted by employers. He's quite involved in gambling and drug use, and is often in trouble with the law. George would most likely fit which of the following personality disorders?

    a. histrionic
    b. borderline
    c. paranoid
    d. antisocial

15. Carol is so unsure of herself that she has passed up opportunities for advancement at work, because she feels she couldn't do the job. Despite the fact that she turned 35 this year, she still lives with her parents, unsure about her ability to take care of herself. She allows other people to make all major decisions in her life, going out of her way to ensure that others like her and won't desert her. Carol would most likely fit which of the following personality disorders?

    a. avoidant
    b. dependent
    c. histrionic
    d. borderline

16. Dave is a loner. He trusts no one, believing that everyone is only "looking out for number one." Even the most harmless actions by others appear suspect to Dave. His relationship of six months' duration ended last month, after he repeatedly accused his partner of unfaithfulness. Dave would most likely fit which of the following personality disorders?

    a. avoidant
    b. antisocial
    c. paranoid
    d. borderline

17. Monica is intensely preoccupied with fears of abandonment. She desperately wants closeness with her partner, but her responses to him are unpredictable. At times she's responded to his attempts at affection with anger and rejection; yet at other times she idealizes him, placing him on a pedestal. She describes her life as empty and often complains that significant people in her life have undermined her attempts at personal growth. Monica would most fit which of the following personality disorders?

    a. avoidant
    b. dependent
    c. histrionic
    d. borderline

18. According to the object-relations approach, treatment of personality disorders should involve

    a. accepting the patient's demanding and manipulative behaviours
    b. challenging the core beliefs of the patient
    c. correcting the flaws in the self resulting from unfortunate formative experiences
    e. all of the above

ANSWERS

FILL-IN-THE-BLANKS

1. inflexible; maladaptive
2. comorbidity; overlap
3. parent-child
4. attachment
5. paranoid
6. schizoid
7. antisocial
8. psychopaths
9. burnout
10. borderline
11. anxious ambivalent
12. histrionic
13. avoidant
14. dependent
15. obsessive-compulsive

MULTIPLE CHOICE

1.	d	10.	c
2.	a	11.	b
3.	c	12.	c
4.	a	13.	b
5.	a	14.	d
6.	c	15.	b
7.	b	16.	c
8.	a	17.	d
9.	d	18.	c

CHAPTER 13

Sexual and Gender Identity Disorders

CHAPTER OUTLINE

LEARNING OBJECTIVES

When you have completed your study of the chapter, you should be able to:

1. Discuss how conceptions of the appropriateness or deviance of sexual behaviours have been influenced by prevailing religious and social views throughout history.

2. Identify and describe the four phases of the sexual response cycle outlined by Masters and Johnson, and compare this with Helen Singer Kaplan's three-stage model.

3. Discuss the role of physical and psychological factors in the following categories of disorders: sexual desire disorders, sexual arousal disorders, orgasmic disorders, premature ejaculation, sexual pain disorders.

4. Outline the basis of psychological interventions for sexual dysfunctions.

5. Describe the various physical treatments used for sexual dysfunctions.

6. Explain how nocturnal penile tumescence can be used to assess whether male erectile disorder is the result of organic or psychological causes.

7. Describe the characteristics and etiology of gender identity disorder.

8. Discuss the pros and cons of sexual reassignment procedures in the treatment of gender identity disorders.

9. Explain what fetishisms are.

10. Describe sadistic and masochistic practices.

11. Explain how exhibitionists, voyeurs, and frotteurs seek sexual excitement, and describe what is known about the characteristics of these offenders.

12. Discuss the common disturbances exhibited by children who have been sexually abused.

13. Discuss the findings of research attempting to identify characteristics that differentiate child molesters from other men.

14. Discuss the results of studies using phallometry to compare the preferences of sexual offenders and normal males.

15. Explain how conditioning theories account for sexual offending.

16. Outline the relation between the four phases in human sexual interactions and specific forms of sexual offending, as suggested by Freund's courtship disorder theory.

17. Discuss how feminist theories conceptualize rape.

18. Explain Marshall and colleagues' comprehensive theory of the etiology of sexual offending.

19. Discuss the advantages of comprehensive programs to the treatment of sexual offenders.

KEY WORDS

Sexual response cycle _____

_____

Lifelong sexual dysfunction _____

_____

Acquired sexual dysfunction _____

_____

Generalized sexual dysfunction _____

_____

Situational sexual dysfunction _____

_____

Hypoactive sexual desire disorder _____

_____

Sexual aversion disorder _____

_____

Female sexual arousal disorder _____

_____

Male erectile disorder _____

_____

Female orgasmic disorder _____

_____

Anorgasmia _____

_____

Male orgasmic disorder _____

_____

Premature ejaculation _____

_____

Dyspareunia _____

_____

Vaginismus _____

_____

Nocturnal penile tumescence _____

_____

Phallometry _____

_____

Prolactin _____

_____

Testosterone _____

_____

Estrogen _____

_____

Performance anxiety _____

_____

Sensate focus _____

_____

Sexual orientation _____

_____

Gender role _____

_____

Gender identity _____

_____

Hermaphroditism _____

_____

Gender identity disorder _____

_____

Gender dysphoria _____

_____

Homosexual gender dysphoria _____

_____

Heterosexual gender dysphoria _____

_____

Paraphilia _____

_____

Egodystonic homosexuality _____

_____

Fetishisms _____

_____

Transvestite _____

_____

Sadists _____

_____

Masochists _____

_____

Hypoxyphilia _____

_____

Autoerotic asphyxia _____

_____

Asphyxiophilia _____

_____

Pedophilia _____

_____

Exhibitionism _____

_____

Voyeurism_____

_____

Frotteurism _____

_____

Courtship disorder theory _____

_____

FILL-IN-THE-BLANKS

1. Masters and Johnson divided the sexual response cycle into four stages: _____, _____, _____, and _____.

2. Shortly after ejaculation, men experience what is called a _____ period, during which they are unresponsive to sexual stimulation.

3. According to DSM-IV, a sexual dysfunction that is of fairly recent onset is said to be an _____ sexual dysfunction.

4. Male erectile disorder used to be referred to as _____; however, this term acquired such negative connotations that it has been abandoned in the official nomenclature.

5. The most common sexual problem presented at clinics is reported to be _____.

6. The persistent involuntary contraction of the muscles in the outer third of the vagina upon attempts at penetration is referred to as _____.

7. Recently, it has been estimated that between one-third and two-thirds of men with erectile failure have some form of _____ impairment.

8. The most common physical treatment for sexual dysfunctions has been _____, for men with erectile disorder.

9. Gender _____ refers to a person's basic sense of self as male or female.

10. _____ is the term that describes rare cases where the individual's reproductive structures are partly female and partly male.

11. A person who wears the clothing of the opposite sex in order to produce or enhance sexual excitement is said to be a _____

12. DSM-IV-TR uses the term _____ to refer to the deliberate induction of oxygen deprivation, terminating, when successful, at orgasm.

13. _____ derive pleasure from touching or rubbing against a nonconsenting person.

14. One characteristic that may distinguish child molesters from other men is a lack of _____ skills.

15. According to Freund's courtship disorder theory, fixation in Stage 1—looking for and appraising a potential partner—would result in _____.

16. _____ theories typically see rape as a nonsexual, or pseudosexual, offence.

MULTIPLE CHOICE

1. During the resolution phase of the sexual response cycle

    a. the genital tissues of both males and females swell as they fill with blood
    b. heart rate increases and breathing becomes more rapid and shallow
    c. rhythmic muscular contractions occur at about eight-second intervals
    d. the body gradually returns to its prearoused state

2. Helen Singer Kaplan proposed a model of sexual stages consisting of

    a. plateau, orgasm, and resolution
    b. desire, excitement, and orgasm
    c. desire, orgasm, and refractory period
    d. excitement, orgasm, and resolution

3. According to DSM-IV-TR, when a problem is apparent only with one partner (e.g., the client's spouse), it is referred to as a

    a. acquired sexual dysfunction   b. generalized sexual dysfunction
    c. situational sexual dysfunction   d. lifelong sexual dysfunction

4. A persistent or recurrent deficiency of sexual fantasies and desire for sex, causing marked distress or interpersonal difficulty, would be labelled

    a. sexual aversion disorder   b. male erectile disorder
    c. hypoactive sexual desire disorder d. male orgasmic disorder

5. The most common sexual complaint of males, although it does not always lead men and their partners to seek treatment, is

    a. premature ejaculation   b. dyspareunia
    c. hermaphroditism   d. hypoactive sexual desire

6. The most commonly reported factor associated with arousal disorders is

   a. hostility
   c. hormonal factors
   b. vascular disease
   d. performance anxiety

7. The most common sexual complaint of men who seek assistance for sexual problems is

   a. premature ejaculation
   c. erectile disorder
   b. dyspareunia
   d. hypoactive sexual desire

8. Psychological sex therapy has been most successful in the treatment of

   a. premature ejaculation and vaginismus
   b. hypoactive sexual desire
   c erectile dysfunction
   d. sexual aversion disorder

9. Heterosexual gender dysphoria differs from homosexual gender dysphoria in that

   a. although both are attracted to the same sex, only homosexual gender dysphorics engage in cross-dressing
   b. although both are attracted to the same sex, only heterosexual gender dysphorics engage in cross-dressing
   c. both homosexual and heterosexual gender dysphorics are attracted to the same sex, and both cross-dress
   d. although both engage in cross-dressing, heterosexual gender dysphorics are attracted to the opposite sex, whereas homosexual gender dysphorics are attracted to the same sex

10. Most transvestites are clearly

    a. heterosexual
    c. hermaphroditic
    b. homosexual
    d. masochistic

11. People who derive sexual pleasure out of experiencing pain or humiliation are referred to as

    a. sadists
    c. egodystonics
    b. frotteurs
    d. masochists

12. The most frequently occurring sexual offence in Western countries is

    a. pedophilia
    c. voyeurism
    b. exhibitionism
    d. frotteurism

13. Which of the following sexual offenders are typically male?

    a. frotteurs
    b. voyeurs
    c. exhibitionists
    d. all of the above

14. Researchers have found that men who molest their own children

    a. are at a lower risk of reoffending than are men who are extrafamilial molesters
    b. are much more severely disturbed than men who molest other people's children
    c. are often much younger than men who molest other people's children
    d. are virtually indistinguishable from men who molest other people's children

15. Which of the following does *not* characterize child molesters?

    a. deficiency in intimacy skills
    b. loneliness
    c. disturbed profiles on measures like the MMPI
    d. frequent emotional or physical rejection/abuse by their own parents

16. According to Freund's courtship disorder theory, frotteurism would be the result of a fixation in

    a. Stage 1 — looking for and appraising a potential partner
    b. Stage 2 — posturing and displaying oneself to the partner
    c. Stage 3 — tactile interaction with the partner
    d. Stage 4 — sexual intercourse

17. Feminist theories of rape emphasize

    a. the offender's apparent anger toward women
    b. conditioning processes in which the association is made between high sexual arousal and an unusual or offensive sexual behaviour
    c. the similarities between animal courtship behaviour and sexual offending
    d. all of the above

18. Which of the following is not a typical component of comprehensive treatment programs for sex offenders?

    a. associating deviant fantasies with a strongly aversive event, such as electric shock
    b. training in social and relationship skills
    c. attempts to overcome the offenders' tendency to deny or minimize their offending
    d. training in empathic skills

ANSWERS

FILL-IN-THE-BLANKS

1. excitement; plateau; orgasm; resolution
2. refractory
3. acquired
4. impotence
5. female orgasmic disorder
6. vaginismus
7. organic
8. physical implants
9. identity
10. hermaphroditism
11. transvestite
12. hypoxyphilia
13. frotteurs
14. intimacy
15. voyeurism
16. feminist

MULTIPLE CHOICE

1.	d	10.	a
2.	b	11.	d
3.	c	12.	b
4.	c	13.	d
5.	a	14.	a
6.	d	15.	c
7.	c	16.	c
8.	a	17.	a
9.	d	18.	a

CHAPTER 14

Developmental Disorders

CHAPTER OUTLINE

MALADAPTIVE BEHAVIOURS AND DUAL DIAGNOSIS

DEINSTITUTIONALIZATION AND COMMUNITY INTEGRATION: HOW EFFECTIVE ARE THEY?

An Acculturation Perspective

Evaluating Quality of Life

PERVASIVE DEVELOPMENTAL DISORDERS: AUTISM

Prevalence

DESCRIPTION

Social Development

Language Acquisition

Attention, Perception, and Cognition

DIAGNOSTIC ISSUES

Asperger Disorder

Child Disintegrative Disorder

Rett Syndrome

Assessment

ETIOLOGY

TREATMENT AND INTERVENTION

Medications and Nutritional Supplements

Behavioural Interventions

LEARNING OBJECTIVES

When you have completed your study of the chapter, you should be able to:

1. Discuss the controversy concerning the use of IQ as the criterion for mental retardation, and explain the importance of assessing adaptive behaviour.

2. Differentiate between the following three types of inheritance, and provide examples of each: dominant, recessive, and sex-linked (or X-linked).

3. Differentiate between three types of Down syndrome.

4. Explain how amniocentesis and chorionic villus sampling are used in prenatal screening for chromosomal abnormalities.

5. Explain the metabolic defect associated with phenylketonuria, and describe how this disorder is commonly treated.

6. Describe each of the following metabolic disorders: congenital hypothyroidism, hyperammonemia, Gaucher's disease, Hurler's syndrome.

7. Describe the effects of prenatal exposure to rubella and to HIV.

8. Describe the physical, cognitive, and behavioural characteristics of fetal alcohol syndrome.

9. Explain what is meant by *cultural-familial retardation*.

10. Explain the developmental-difference controversy.

11. Discuss what twin, adoption, and deprivation studies reveal concerning the roles of genetic and environmental factors in intellectual development.

12. Describe the results of early intervention programs.

13. Describe the physical and psychological characteristics of Down syndrome.

14. Describe the physical and psychological characteristics of Fragile X syndrome.

15. Discuss the effects of developmental disorders on the family.

16. Discuss the issues of sexual activity and parenting in people with developmental disabilities.

17. Describe the most frequent aberrant behaviours that co-occur with developmental disabilities.

18. Explain the relevance of the acculturation framework to evaluating the effects of deinstitutionalization.

19. Describe the social deficits that characterize autism.

20. Explain the deficits in language acquisition that are characteristic of autism.

21. Discuss the deficits in attention, perception, and cognition associated with autism.

22. Describe the symptoms of Asperger disorder, and explain how this disorder differs from autism.

23. Describe the four stages of cognitive and functional deterioration that characterize Rett syndrome.

24. Discuss the two major hypotheses—psychogenic and biological—concerning the etiology of autism.

25. Discuss the effectiveness of medications and nutritional supplements in the treatment of autism.

26. Describe the behavioural methods that have been used with autistic children.

27. Outline three major components commonly found in definitions of learning disabilities.

28. Define each of the following learning disabilities: dyslexia, dyscalculia, and dysgraphia.

KEY WORDS

Stereotypy _____

_____

Developmental handicap _____

_____

Developmental disability _____

_____

Mental retardation _____

_____

Down syndrome _____

_____

Trisomy 21 _____

_____

Translocation _____

_____

Mosaicism _____

_____

Amniocentesis _____

_____

Chorionic villus sampling (CVS) _____

_____

Phenylketonuria (PKU) _____

_____

Rubella _____

_____

HIV _____

_____

Fetal alcohol syndrome (FAS) _____

_____

Fetal alcohol effects (FAE) _____

_____

Thalidomide _____

_____

Cultural-familial retardation _____

_____

Developmental-difference controversy _____

_____

Contact hypothesis _____

_____

Diagnostic overshadowing _____

_____

Dual diagnosis _____

_____

Normalization principle _____

_____

Deinstitutionalization _____

_____

Acculturation framework _____

_____

Quality of life _____

_____

Autism _____

_____

Pervasive developmental disorders _____

_____

Echolalia _____

_____

Pronoun reversal _____

_____

Savants _____

_____

Asperger disorder _____

_____

Child disintegrative disorder (CDD) _____

_____

Rett syndrome _____

_____

Facilitated communication (FC) _____

_____

Learning disorders _____

_____

Dyslexia _____

_____

Dyscalculia _____

_____

Dysgraphia _____

_____

FILL-IN-THE-BLANKS

1. Sex-linked, or X-linked, disorders primarily affect _____ *(males/females)*.

2. Phenylketonuria is a disorder associated with the _____ pattern of inheritance.

3. The best known chromosomal abnormality associated with mental retardation is _____.

4. Whereas individuals with Down syndrome due to _____ have all the features found in trisomy 21, people with _____ Down syndrome may have fewer physical characteristics, better speech, and higher intellectual functioning.

5. _____ is a recently developed prenatal screening test that involves obtaining cells from the placenta. It can be carried out as early as the 10th to 12th week of pregnancy.

6. In PKU, a liver enzyme is inactive, causing an inability to process or metabolize the amino acid _____.

7. _____ is a metabolic disorder that involves a deficiency in the enzyme that normally transforms the neurotoxic ammonia into urea, which is excreted into the urine.

8. _____ is the term used to describe children who display some of the symptoms of fetal alcohol syndrome, without meeting all the diagnostic criteria.

9. Adults with Down syndrome are at high risk for _____-type dementia.

10. Fragile X syndrome occurs more frequently in _____ *(males/females)*.

11. Fragile X syndrome is the most common _____ cause of mental retardation.

12. Since the 1970s, services for people with developmental disabilities have been guided by the _____ principle, which has contributed to the deinstitutionalization of thousands.

13. Viewed within the acculturation framework, the normalization approach might be considered as _____.

14. Autism is the best known of the _____ developmental disorders.

15. One of the most common characteristics of speech in children with autism is _____, in which the child will repeat another person's words, using the same or similar intonation.

16. A small proportion of people with autism, often called _____, display islets of exceptional ability in areas such as mathematics, music, art, or memory.

17. _____ is characterized by a unique pattern of cognitive and functional deterioration that has been divided into four stages.

18. Biologically based treatments for autism _____ *(have/have not)* been found to be generally effective.

19. Disorders of written expression, or _____, are characterized by limited handwriting skills as well as spelling, grammatical, and punctuation errors.

MULTIPLE CHOICE

1. The mild range of mental retardation is defined as IQ scores falling between

   a. 80–85 to approximately 100   b. 70–75 to approximately 85
   c. 50–55 to approximately 70   d. 35–40 to approximately 50

2. Which of the following is *not* a criticism of the use of IQ tests as the primary means of diagnosing mental retardation?

   a. The test-retest reliability of most IQ tests is not particularly high.
   b. IQ tests were not devised to take into account sensory, motor, and language deficits, which may contribute to poor performance.
   c. The test situation may be unfamiliar and overwhelming, which may limit performance.
   d. It is questionable whether scores in the lower end of the scale are meaningful because some major IQ tests were not standardized on people with developmental disabilities.

3. Which of the following is not among the abilities assessed by the Vineland Adaptive Behavior Scales?

    a. communication
    b. IQ
    c. socialization
    d. motor skills

4. Three types of inheritance are

    a. dominant, submissive, X-linked
    b. dominant, recessive, Y-linked
    c. dominant, submissive, Y-linked
    d. dominant, recessive, X-linked

5. Which of the following is an example of a disorder associated with dominant inheritance?

    a. phenylketonuria
    b. Fragile X syndrome
    c. tuberous sclerosis
    d. Tay-Sachs disease

6. The least common type of Down syndrome is

    a. trisomy 21
    b. mosaicism
    c. translocation
    d. fragile-21

7. Amniocentesis is a procedure to screen for chromosomal abnormalities that is conducted

    a. immediately following conception
    b. between the 8th and 12th weeks of pregnancy
    c. within the first few hours after birth
    d. between the 11th and 18th weeks of pregnancy

8. The treatment most frequently used with phenylketonuria is

    a. social skills training
    b. medications that regulate levels of neurotransmitters
    c. facilitated communication
    d. dietary restrictions

9. Symptoms of fetal alcohol syndrome include

   a. deafness and heart disease
   b. lack of social responsiveness and stereotyped behaviours
   c. prenatal and postnatal growth retardation and central nervous system dysfunction
   d. echolalia and pronoun reversal

10. In approximately 75% of people diagnosed as having a developmental handicap

    a. no organic cause or brain dysfunction has been identified
    b. chromosomal abnormalities, particularly in Down syndrome, are the cause of the handicap
    c. the prenatal environment, especially the consequences of alcohol and drug use, is responsible for the handicap
    d. genetic abnormalities are the cause of the handicap

11. Generally, the IQ scores of adopted children tend to be

    a. more similar to those of their adoptive parents than to those of their biological parents
    b. more similar to those of their biological parents than to those of their adoptive parents
    c. approximately equally similar to those of both their adopted and their biological parents
    d. dissimilar to both those of their adopted and their biological parents

12. Research conducted with infants and children adopted from Romanian orphanages indicates that

    a. environmental enrichment can clearly reverse the consequences of early deprivation
    b. the severe consequences of early deprivation cannot be undone by later environmental enrichment
    c. environmental enrichment can produce positive effects, which may depend on the extent of deprivation experienced by the child
    d. as long as children's physical needs were met in the orphanage, social deprivation was of little consequence to their development

13. _____ is the second most frequently occurring chromosomal abnormality causing mental retardation.

    a. phenylketonuria
    b. Tay-Sachs disease
    c. galactosemia
    d. Fragile X syndrome

14. The co-occurrence of serious behavioural or psychiatric disorders in people with developmental disabilities has been labelled

    a. diagnostic overshadowing
    b. the developmental-difference controversy
    c. the contact hypothesis
    d. dual diagnosis

15. Viewed within the acculturation framework, traditional institutional care could be considered

    a. assimilation
    b. integration
    c. marginalization
    d. segregation

16. Autism occurs three to four times as often in _____, although the difference appears only among people with _____ IQs.

    a. females; lower
    b males; lower
    c. females; higher
    d. males; higher

17. Two critical features of autism are

    a. characteristic facial abnormalities; learning disabilities
    b. extremely low IQ; islets of exceptional ability in specific areas
    c. social dysfunction; unusual responses to the environment
    d. communication dysfunction; a pattern of cognitive and functional deterioration

18. The disorder that has been generally viewed as a mild version of autism, associated with higher intellectual functioning is

    a. Rett syndrome
    b. Asperger disorder
    c. child disintegrative disorder
    d. Tay-Sachs disease

19. Proponents of the psychogenic approach described parents of children with autism as

    a. above average intelligence, overprotective, and indulging
    b. below average in intelligence, authoritarian, and overcontrolling
    c. of average intelligence, permissive, and warm
    d. highly intelligent, rigid, and lacking in warmth

20. Dyslexia

    a. involves problems recognizing and understanding numerical symbols, sequencing problems, and attentional deficits
    b. involves difficulties not only in the recognition but also in the comprehension of words
    c. is characterized by limited handwriting skills and spelling, grammatical, and punctuation errors
    d. both b and c

ANSWERS

FILL-IN-THE-BLANKS

1. males
2. recessive
3. Down syndrome
4. translocation; mosaic
5. chorionic villus sampling
6. phenylalanine
7. hyperammonemia
8. Fetal alcohol effects
9. Alzheimer
10. males
11. hereditary
12. normalization
13. integration
14. pervasive
15. echolalia
16. savants
17. Rett syndrome
18. have not
19. dysgraphia

MULTIPLE CHOICE

1. c
2. a
3. b
4. d
5. c
6. b
7. d
8. d
9. c
10. a
11. b
12. c
13. d
14. d
15. d
16. d
17. c
18. b
19. d
20. b

CHAPTER 15

Behaviour and Emotional Disorders of Childhood and Adolescence

CHAPTER OUTLINE

HISTORICAL VIEWS OF CHILDHOOD

Developmental Psychopathology

Risk and Protective Factors

Assessing and Treating Children: Special Issues

Prevalence of Childhood Disorders

ATTENTION DEFICIT /HYPERACTIVITY DISORDER

Historical Perspective

Diagnosis

Long-Term Development

Etiology

Treatment

OPPOSITIONAL DEFIANT DISORDER AND CONDUCT DISORDER

Oppositional Defiant Disorder: Description

Conduct Disorder: Description

Diagnostic Issues

Etiology

Long-Term Development

Treatment

SEPARATION ANXIETY DISORDER (SAD)

    Diagnosis and Assessment

    Long-Term Development

    Etiology

    Treatment

LEARNING OBJECTIVES

When you have completed your study of the chapter, you should be able to:

1. Describe the principles endorsed by developmental psychopathology.

2. Explain the differences between children and adults in seeking professional help. Describe the limitations in the assessment and treatment of children's disorders.

3. Explain the difference between externalizing and internalizing disorders.

4. Describe and discuss the findings of the Ontario Child Health Study.

5. Describe the DSM-IV-TR diagnostic criteria for ADHD.

6. Discuss the comorbidity rates of ADHD with other disorders.

7. Describe and explain the results of long-term follow-up studies with ADHD children.

8. Discuss the various explanations that have been offered concerning the causes of ADHD.

9. Discuss the effectiveness of medication and of behavioural and psychological treatments for ADHD.

10. Compare the diagnostic criteria for oppositional defiant disorder and conduct disorder.

11. Discuss the roles that family factors may play in the etiology of conduct disorders.

12. Describe the long-term development of CD in boys and girls.

13. Identify and describe the major treatment methods for ODD and CD.

14. Describe and discuss the effectiveness of the Community Parent Education Program (COPE) in treating conduct disorder.

15. Describe the DSM-IV-TR criteria for a diagnosis of separation anxiety disorder (SAD).

16. Discuss the role of family factors, temperament, and attachment in the etiology of SAD.

17. Describe the three major methods of therapy used to treat SAD in children.

KEY WORDS

Developmental psychopathology _____

_____

Risk factor _____

_____

SSRIs _____

_____

Externalizing problems _____

_____

Internalizing problems _____

_____

Ontario Child Health Study (OCHS) _____

_____

Attention deficit/hyperactivity disorder (ADHD)_____

_____

Minimal brain dysfunction (MBD)   _____

_____

Methylphenidate (Ritalin)_____

_____

Dextroamphetamine (Dexedrine) _____

_____

Oppositional defiant disorder (ODD) _____

_____

Conduct disorder (CD)   _____

_____

Life-course-persistent _____

_____

Adolescent-limited   _____

_____

Problem-solving skills training   _____

_____

Parent training (PT)   _____

_____

Family therapy   _____

_____

Community Parent Education Program (COPE) _____

Separation anxiety disorder (SAD) _____

_____

_____

Relational aggression _____

_____

Intergenerational transmission of risk _____

_____

FILL-IN-THE-BLANKS

1. According to the principles of developmental psychopathology, abnormal behaviour is _____.

2. Loeber describes a _____ factor as an event occurring early in a child's life that is predictive of a later outcome.

3. In DSM-IV-TR, childhood disorders referred to by professionals as behaviour problems, externalizing problems, and problems of undercontrol are found under _____ Disorders.

4. In the mid-1880s a German physician named Heinrich Hoffman wrote a poem entitled "The Story of Fidgety Phillipe" in which he described a _____ child.

5. According to DSM-IV-TR, there are three essential features of ADHD: age-inappropriate levels of _____, _____, and _____.

6. In adolescence, approximately 25% of ADHD children will meet the diagnostic criteria for _____ and _____.

7. _____ is the most efficient means of treating the behaviours of ADHD.

8. The most frequently prescribed stimulant for controlling ADHD behaviours is _____.

9. _____ is the greatest concern for children diagnosed with conduct disorder.

10. Attempts to establish a single, ultimate cause for the behaviour patterns of CD are probably futile. Rather, _____—that is, the understanding that people and their environments affect one other—is likely to offer a more accurate explanation.

11. _____ training for CD usually combines several different procedures, including modelling and practice, role-playing, and reinforcement contingencies.

12. In treating conduct disorder, parent training programs are based on a _____ causal model.

13. The reciprocal rewarding, between parent and child, of undesirable or inappropriate behaviour has been described as the _____ process.

14. Economic analyses have shown that COPE is six times as _____ than individual parent training programs.

15. Although the onset for separation anxiety disorder (SAD) may occur as early as the preschool years, the average age of children presenting at clinics is about _____.

16. There is speculation that children with separation anxiety disorder may be at risk for _____ and panic disorder in adulthood.

17. According to Kagan and his colleagues, children who are behaviourally _____ show a profound avoidance of others in preschool and demonstrate atypical autonomic nervous system responses in the face of novelty.

18. In _____, a child is exposed to a wide variety of toys, artistic materials, and dolls, usually chosen by a therapist and based on suspected problems.

19. Psychotropic medication _____ (*has/has not*) consistently demonstrated evidence of usefulness with SAD patients.

MULTIPLE CHOICE

1. All of the following are disorders studied by the Ontario Child Health Study, *except*

    a. CD
    b. hyperactivity
    c. Asperger disorder
    d. somatization

2. The largest numbers of children seen in mental health clinics are those diagnosed with

    a. behavioural inhibition
    b. minimal brain dysfunction
    c. attention deficit/hyperactivity disorder
    d. oppositional defiant disorder

3. The first designation for ADHD to be accepted by professionals was

    a. hyperkinetic reaction
    b. minimal brain dysfunction
    c. disruptive behaviour disorder
    d. hyperactive disorder

4. Among Ontario schoolchildren, the percentage of children diagnosed with ADHD that also qualify for a diagnosis of conduct disorder is

    a. 15%
    b. 25%
    c. 40%
    d. 50%

5. In adults with childhood onset of ADHD, Zametkin et al. (1990) found reduced glucose metabolism, indicating less brain activity during

    a. auditory attention tasks
    b. visual perception tasks
    c. problem-solving tasks
    d. motor sensory tasks

6. Although medication may improve behaviour, ADHD children may need additional special help to improve

    a. academic achievement   b. social behaviour
    c. classroom behaviour   d. attention

7. All of the following are forms of treatment for ODD and CD, *except*

    a. problem-solving skills training
    b. parent training
    c. stimulant medication
    d. family therapy

8. It has been found that mothers of children with conduct disorder are more likely than mothers of control children

    a. to be poor at supervising their child and inconsistent in applying discipline
    b. to be quite punitive, in a consistent fashion, in disciplining their children
    c. to be highly accepting, warm, and affectionate with their children
    d. all of the above

9. All of the following are goals of functional family therapy, *except*

    a. to increase reciprocity
    b. to increase problem-solving skills
    c. to establish clear communication
    d. to identify solutions to interpersonal problems

10. Which of the following is *not* an area in which deficits have been found in children with CD?

    a. problem-solving skills
    b. social perception
    c. reaction to novelty or challenge
    d. social attributions

11. All of the following are found in the etiology of both CD and SAD, *except*

    a. attachment
    b. family links
    c. neurological signs
    d. temperament

12. After revisions from DSM-III-R, only SAD remained in DSM-IV-TR as a

    a. childhood anxiety disorder
    b. childhood disorder
    c. childhood affective disorder
    d. childhood disruptive disorder

13. Fears differ at different ages. When asked about their anxieties, five- to eight-year-olds most often report

    a. worries about harm befalling a parent
    b. physical complaints on school days
    c. excessive distress upon parental separation
    d. fear of novelty or challenge

14. SAD may sometimes be misdiagnosed because the parents describe the child as being quite _____. However, it is usually found that the behaviour is restricted to anxiety-provoking situations that involve separation from the parents.

    a. hyperactive
    b. depressed
    c. oppositional
    d. aloof

15. Which of the following is true concerning sex differences in SAD?

    a. Research has shown that SAD occurs more frequently in boys.
    b. Research has shown that SAD occurs more frequently in girls.
    c. Research has generally not revealed sex differences in SAD.
    d. None of the above is true.

16. A child who shows profound avoidance of others in preschool and demonstrates atypical autonomous nervous system responses to novelty, displays what is called

    a. behavioural inhibition
    b. externalization
    c. problems of undercontrol
    d. ADHD

17. A widely used medication to treat SAD is

    a. dextroamphetamine
    b. methylphenidate
    c. pemoline
    d. benzodiazepines

18. A therapeutic approach that tries to teach better communication and interpersonal skills is

    a. family therapy
    b. parent training
    c. cognitive behavioural training
    d. all of the above

ANSWERS

FILL-IN-THE-BLANKS

1. multidetermined
2. risk
3. Disruptive Behaviour
4. hyperactive
5. inattention; impulsivity; hyperactivity
6. antisocial personality disorder; alcohol use disorder
7. stimulant medication
8. methylphenidate (Ritalin)
9. aggression
10. reciprocal determinism
11. problem-solving
12. social learning
13. coercive
14. cost-effective
15. nine years
16. agoraphobia
17. inhibited
18. play therapy
19. has not

MULTIPLE CHOICE

1.	c	10.	c
2.	c	11.	c
3.	b	12.	a
4.	c	13.	a
5.	a	14.	c
6.	a	15.	c
7.	c	16.	a
8.	a	17.	d
9.	b	18.	d

CHAPTER 16

Mental Disorders and Aging

CHAPTER OUTLINE

LEARNING OBJECTIVES

When you have completed your study of the chapter, you should be able to:

1. Discuss why mental disorders in the elderly warrant special attention.

2. Discuss the issue of loss and vulnerability in the elderly.

3. Discuss several common myths about aging and mental disorders.

4. Explain why epidemiological information likely underestimates the prevalence of mental disorders for older adults.

5. Explain the social breakdown/social reconstruction framework.

6. Describe the differences in how activity theory and disengagement theory view successful aging. How do personality factors interact with activity level?

7. Explain how successful aging may entail selective optimization with compensation.

8. Discuss the factors that increase the risk of suicide in the elderly.

9. Explain why it can be difficult to diagnose major depressive disorder (MDD) in the elderly. How are the symptoms of MDD different in older than in younger adults?

10. Discuss the common methods of treating MDD in older adults. How effective are they, and what are their drawbacks?

11. Describe five factors that must be considered before a diagnosis of primary sleep disorder can be made.

12. Describe three normal age-related changes in sleeping patterns.

13. Discuss both the nocturnal and daytime symptoms of primary insomnia.

14. What are the drawbacks of pharmacological treatments for primary insomnia?

15. What are some behavioural and cognitive strategies for dealing with insomnia?

16. Describe the symptoms and treatment of nocturnal myoclonus.

17. Describe three types of sleep apnea, and explain how this disorder can be treated.

18. Describe three types of anxiety disorders common in the elderly.

19. Explain how late-onset schizophrenia differs from early-onset schizophrenia.

20. What is delusional disorder, and how does it differ from schizophrenia?

21. Describe the characteristics of and treatment for delirium.

22. Discuss the differences between primary dementia and secondary dementia. How do these differ from pseudodementias?

23. Outline the five diagnostic criteria for mild cognitive impairment proposed by Ronald Petersen of the Mayo Clinic.

24. Describe the characteristics of the early, middle, and late stages of Alzheimer's disease.

25. Describe the differences in the brains of Alzheimer's victims and normal old people.

26. What evidence is there for a genetic basis to Alzheimer's? What are some other hypothesized causes of Alzheimer's?

27. Discuss how Alzheimer's may be treated.

28. Describe the cause and symptoms of vascular dementia.

29. Discuss the characteristics and causes of the following forms of dementias:

   Lewy body dementia

   Frontotemporal dementia

KEY WORDS

Normal aging _____

_____

Polypharmacy _____

_____

Point prevalence _____

_____

Social breakdown _____

_____

Social reconstruction _____

_____

Activity theory _____

_____

Disengagement theory _____

_____

Primary insomnia _____

_____

Nocturnal myoclonus _____

_____

Sleep apnea _____

_____

Late-onset schizophrenia _____

_____

Delusional disorder _____

_____

Dementia _____

_____

Pseudodementia _____

_____

Mild cognitive impairment _____

_____

Alzheimer's disease _____

_____

Vascular dementia_____

_____

Lewy body dementia _____

_____

Frontotemporal dementia _____

_____

FILL-IN-THE-BLANKS

1. Even if the majority of older people have a pathological condition, that does not mean that the condition is normal, only that it is _____.

2. The percentage of people in a particular age group who currently have a disorder is referred to as the _____ for that age group.

3. _____ theory holds that people who age successfully are those who maintain the same activity level they had in middle age.

4. According to one recently developed theoretical framework, old age brings losses of abilities and skills. Successful aging entails _____ remaining skills and _____ where possible for reduced abilities.

5. When either major depressive disorder or bipolar disorder occur for the first time later in life, hereditary factors are _____ (more/less) likely to be a primary cause than when either occurs earlier.

6. In contrast to patients of younger ages, elderly MDD patients are significantly _____ (more/less) likely to be treated with psychotherapy and significantly _____ (more/less) likely to receive pharmacotherapy and ECT.

7. _____ are the most common treatments for primary insomnia.

8. The second most common sleep disorder in older adults is _____.

9. Snoring is an indication of a blockage of the upper airways, which is the cause of _____ apnea.

10. The characteristic feature of delusional disorder is the presence of one or more delusions that last for at least _____.

11. For a long time, dementia was commonly known as _____ because the mental deterioration was thought to be simply the result of the normal aging process.

12. Disorders that produce cognitive impairment but that can be reversed are referred to as _____.

13. The most common type of dementia is _____.

14. The second most common form of dementia in Canada is _____ dementia, accounting for about 18% of cases.

15. A key pathological change in the brains of Parkinson's disease patients are filaments of protein with a dense core that are called _____.

16. Compared with Alzheimer's, age of onset in frontotemporal dementia tends to be _____ and its course appears to be _____.

MULTIPLE CHOICE

1. By definition, things that are pathological cannot be

   a. normal
   c. common

   b. typical
   d. accepted

2. Which of the following is true?

   a. The development of pathology must be accepted as a part of normal aging.
   b. Older adults do not respond well to treatment for mental disorders.
   c. The longer one lives, the greater the likelihood of experiencing those conditions that trigger pathology.
   d. All of the above are true.

3. Disengagement theory holds that successful aging involves

   a. accepting that it is normal and natural to slow down as people move into old age
   b. replacing more strenuous activities with ones that are less strenuous while maintaining the same level of activity that one had in middle age
   c. dealing with loss of abilities and skills by optimizing remaining skills and compensating where possible for reduced abilities
   d. intervening in the social breakdown cycle and starting a cycle of social reconstruction

4. Which of the following increases the risk of suicide in older individuals?

   a. being female
   b. having a higher income
   c. being divorced or widowed
   d. being Canadian

5. Both dysthymic disorder and major depressive disorder are more common

   a. in younger than in older adults, and more common in men than in women
   b. in younger than in older adults, and more common in women than in men
   c. in older than in younger adults, and more common in men than in women
   d. in older than in younger adults, and more common in women than in men

6. Older individuals with MDD, in contrast to younger individuals, are more likely to report

   a. feelings of worthlessness
   b. guilt
   c. weight loss and other somatic symptoms
   d. all of the above

7. Which of the following is not among the three most common anxiety disorders in older adults?

   a. posttraumatic stress disorder
   b. social phobia
   c. specific phobias
   d. generalized anxiety disorder

8. Which of the following are normal age-related changes in sleeping patterns?

   a. changes in EEG activity
   b. changes in the organization of sleep stages
   c. changes in circadian rhythms
   d. all of the above

9. Nocturnal myoclonus is characterized by

   a. episodes of breathing cessation while sleeping that last about 10 seconds
   b. both nocturnal and daytime symptoms
   c. periodic leg movements during sleep that sometimes wake the individual
   d. low blood oxygen saturation and awakenings from sleep

10. Which of the following is *not* useful in treating sleep apnea?

   a. hypnotic medications
   b. respiratory stimulants
   c. avoiding sleeping on one's back
   d. losing weight

11. People with late-onset schizophrenia are more likely than those with early-onset schizophrenia to have

   a. disorganized speech
   b. lack of logical thought
   c. flattened affect
   d. florid and bizarre delusions and hallucinations

12. Which of the following is *not* among the diagnostic criteria for delusional disorder?

   a. delusions that are bizarre in nature
   b. lack of marked impairment in functioning
   c. no evidence to suggest that there is a chemical or medical cause of the symptoms
   d. actually, *all* of the above are diagnostic criteria for delusional disorder

13. The hallmark symptom of delirium is

    a. persecutory delusions
    b. progressive cognitive deterioration
    c. reduced or clouded consciousness
    d. all of the above

14. Which of the following is *not* a diagnostic criterion for mild cognitive impairment?

    a. memory complaints that are corroborated by family or other informants
    b. no dementia
    c. impaired social and occupational functioning
    d. otherwise normal cognitive functioning

15. Research with Alzheimer's clearly indicates

    a. the presence of an Alzheimer's gene on chromosome 21
    b. that its etiology is physiological in basis
    c. that a slow virus is likely involved in its etiology
    d. that most individuals who develop this dementia also suffer from Down syndrome

16. The second most common cause of dementia is

    a. Alzheimer's disease
    b. Down syndrome
    c. Creutzfeldt-Jakob disease
    d. cerebrovascular damage

17. Which of the following is *not* a difference between Lewy body dementia and AD and vascular dementia?

    a. spontaneous features of Parkinsonism, including slowed body movement, muscle rigidity, resting tremor, and postural instability
    b. a progressive cognitive decline that interferes with social or occupational functioning
    c. neuroleptic sensitivity
    d. recurrent well-formed hallucinations

18. Which of the following is characteristic of patients with frontotemporal dementia?

    a. They often have relatively intact memory function until later in the disease process.
    b. They may develop a taste for sweet foods and engage in overeating.
    c. They may exhibit striking behaviour changes, such as disinhibition, impulsiveness, repetitiveness, and so on.
    d. All of the above.

ANSWERS

FILL-IN-THE-BLANKS

1. typical
2. point prevalence
3. activity
4. optimizing; compensating
5. less
6. less; more
7. sedatives or hypnotics
8. nocturnal myoclonus
9. obstructive
10. one month
11. senility (or senile dementia)
12. pseudodementias
13 Alzheimer's disease
14 vascular
15 Lewy bodies
16. younger; variable

MULTIPLE CHOICE

1.	a	10.	a
2.	c	11.	d
3.	a	12.	a
4.	c	13.	c
5.	b	14.	c
6.	c	15.	b
7.	a	16.	d
8.	d	17.	b
9.	c	18.	d

CHAPTER 17

Therapies

CHAPTER OUTLINE

EVALUATING THE EFFECTS OF PSYCHOTHERAPY

LEARNING OBJECTIVES

When you have completed your study of the chapter, you should be able to:

1. Describe the major benefits and side effects of antipsychotic medications.

2. Describe the advantages and disadvantages of anxiolytic medication.

3. Identify and describe the three major categories of antidepressant medication.

4. Describe the uses and drawbacks of lithium and of stimulant medication.

5. Identify and describe the five basic techniques upon which classic psychoanalysts rely.

6. Explain how each of the following psychodynamic therapies differs from psychoanalysis:

   Brief psychodynamic psychotherapy

   Ego analysis

   Adler's individual psychology

   Interpersonal psychodynamic therapy

   Time-limited dynamic psychotherapy

7. Explain the basic assumptions, characteristics, and goals of the client-centred, existential, and Gestalt approaches to psychotherapy.

8. Explain how cognitive-behavioural therapists approach psychotherapy.

9. Briefly describe each of the following cognitive-behavioural interventions:

   Reinforcement

   Response shaping

   Behavioural activation

   Exposure

   Assertiveness training

Problem solving

Self-instructional training

Cognitive restructuring

10. Identify the three ingredients that, according to Jerome Frank, are similarities between different approaches to psychotherapy.

11. Discuss the various treatment modalities described in the chapter—individual therapy, couples therapy, family therapy, and group therapy.

12. Discuss what surveys have shown concerning each of the following:

Who provides psychotherapy?

Who seeks psychotherapy?

Duration of treatment

13. Explain the distinction between treatment efficacy and treatment effectiveness.

14. Explain what meta-analysis is. Describe how this procedure has been used in the evaluation of the effectiveness of psychotherapy.

15. Based on the results of meta-analytic studies, what conclusions can be drawn about the effectiveness of various forms of psychotherapy?

16. Indicate the interventions that have been found most effective with each of the following disorders:

   Anxiety disorders

   Mood disorders

   Childhood disorders

   Sleep disorders

   Axis II disorders

17. Discuss the relation between duration of treatment and effectiveness of treatment.

18. Discuss the issue of evidence-based practice.

19. What are the advantages and problems associated with "self-help" strategies?

KEY WORDS

Psychoactive agents _____

_____

Extrapyramidal effects _____

_____

Transference _____

_____

Ego analysts _____

_____

Interpersonal psychodynamic psychotherapy _____

_____

Time-limited dynamic psychotherapy (TLDP) _____

_____

Therapeutic alliance _____

_____

Client-centred therapy_____

_____

Process-experiential therapy _____

_____

Response shaping _____

_____

Exposure therapy _____

_____

Systematic desensitization _____

_____

Problem-solving approach _____

_____

Self-instructional training _____

_____

Cognitive restructuring _____

_____

Emotionally focused therapy _____

_____

Reframing _____

_____

Treatment efficacy _____

_____

Treatment effectiveness _____

_____

Meta-analysis _____

_____

Effect size _____

_____

Evidence-based practice _____

_____

Empirically supported therapy _____

_____

Empirically supported therapy relationships _____

_____

Clinical practice guidelines _____

_____

FILL-IN-THE-BLANKS

1. ECT was originally developed as a treatment for _____.

2. A _____ is an inert substance that is associated with alleviation of symptoms through expectancy effects.

3. _____, which is characterized by strange muscular movements, such as eye twitching and tongue thrusting, is a side effect of prolonged administration of anti-psychotic medications

4. _____ has long been the treatment of choice for bipolar disorder, although recent years have seen an increase in the use of newer antipsychotic medications.

5. In dream analysis, it is the psychoanalyst's task to distinguish between the _____ content of the dream (which is consciously remembered by the client), and the more important _____ content (the unconscious ideas and impulses that have been disguised).

6. Like psychoanalysts, _____ therapists also interpret dreams, looking to the importance that the dream has to the client at that moment.

7. Because many new skills are acquired gradually, the behavioural technique known as _____ is used to shape behaviour in gradual steps toward a goal.

8. The essence of _____ in the treatment of depression is to help patients develop strategies to increase their overall activity and to counteract their tendencies to avoid activities.

9. In _____, fear-inducing stimuli are arranged in a hierarchy. Individuals gradually progress through the hierarchy in their imagination, while maintaining a relaxed state.

10. The _____ approach involves using techniques stemming from diverse orientations, while the _____ approach involves developing a conceptual model to guide treatment based on elements of diverse orientations.

11. _____ is a method used to quantitatively review previous research.

12. It is now commonly accepted that treatment for specific phobias must involve an element of _____.

13. The symptoms of attention deficit/hyperactivity disorder, oppositional defiant disorder, and conduct disorder can be substantially reduced through treatments that focus on improving the parents' _____ skills.

14. The most widely studied couple therapy is _____ marital therapy.

MULTIPLE CHOICE

1. ECT is still used to treat severe _____ that has (have) not responded to other treatments.

   a. schizophrenia
   b. phobias
   c. mania
   d. depression

2. In a _____, patients are unaware of whether they are receiving medication or placebo, but the therapist is aware.

   a. double-blind trial
   b. randomized clinical trial
   c. placebo washout
   d. single-blind trial

3. Anti-Parkinsonian drugs have been found to relieve certain of the extrapyramidal effects that may be associated with

   a. antipsychotic medications
   b. anxiolytics
   c. antidepressant medications
   d. lithium

4. Xanax (alprazolam) and Ativan (lorazepam) are examples of

   a. antipsychotics
   b. anxiolytics
   c. SSRIs
   d. mood stabilizers

5. Prozac, Zoloft, and Paxil are well-known examples of

   a. MAOIs
   b. Tricyclics
   c. SSRIs
   d. mood stabilizers

6. Common foods, such as yeast, chocolate, and beer, that contain the enzyme tyramine can cause a life-threatening increase in blood pressure if taken in combination with

   a. selective serotonin reuptake inhibitors
   b. lithium
   c. monoamine oxidase inhibitors
   d. tricyclics

7. The class of drugs most commonly used in the treatment of children with attention deficit/hyperactivity disorder is

   a. benzodiazepines
   b. phenothiazines
   c. SSRIs
   d. stimulants

8. The core of psychoanalytic therapy is _____, which occurs when the client responds to the therapist as he or she responded to significant figures from his or her childhood (generally the parents).

   a. association
   b. resistance
   c. acceptance
   d. transference

9. Alfred Adler proposed that sexual and aggressive instincts are less important than

   a. the individual's striving to overcome personal weakness
   b. the individual's potential for growth and for making choices
   c. the individual's awareness of his or her genuine feelings
   d. the stunting of personal growth that results from judgments imposed by others

10. Interpersonal psychodynamic psychotherapy was developed by _____, who believed that mental disorders resulted from maladaptive early interactions between child and parent.

    a. Erik Erikson
    b. Harry Stack Sullivan
    c. Karen Horney
    d. Alfred Adler

11. Client-centred therapy emphasizes

    a. the warmth and permissiveness of the therapist
    b. the uniqueness of each individual
    c. distortions that exist in the person's awareness of his or her genuine feelings
    d. distortions in the individual's perceptions of events

12. In vivo exposure is a technique that relies on the behavioural principle of

    a. response shaping
    b. extinction
    c. aversion
    d. skills training

13. Donald Meichenbaum from the University of Waterloo developed _____ training to coach individuals in effective strategies for talking themselves through difficult challenges.

    a. desensitization
    b. assertiveness
    c. self-instructional
    d. biofeedback

14. Both Albert Ellis's rational emotive therapy and Aaron Beck's cognitive therapy are based on the assumption that an individual's adjustment is affected by

    a. his or her perception of events, rather than the events themselves
    b. his or her striving to overcome personal weakness
    c. judgments imposed on the individual by others that stunt the individual's growth
    d. past and present choices made by the individual

15. Which of the following is *not* among the three central ingredients in therapy described by Jerome Frank?

    a. an expectation, conveyed by the therapist, to think, act, and feel in a different way
    b. an expectation of hope conveyed to the client by the therapist
    c. a firm demand to "shape up" conveyed to the client by the therapist
    d. an alternative explanation for the problem presented to the client

16. The majority of people who receive psychotherapy attend

    a. fewer than 6 sessions
    b. between 25 and 50 sessions, on average
    c. fewer than 10 sessions
    d. between 15 and 20 sessions

17. Which of the following is a highly effective treatment for panic disorder?

    a. exposure and response prevention
    b. cognitive restructuring and thought-stopping
    c. cognitive restructuring and interoceptive exposure
    d. cognitive therapy and reminiscence therapy

18. Research suggests that both _____ and _____ are effective in treating depression.

    a. psychoanalysis; Gestalt therapy
    b. client-centred therapy; existential therapy
    c. exposure; response prevention
    d. interpersonal psychotherapy; cognitive therapy

ANSWERS

FILL-IN-THE-BLANKS

1. schizophrenia
2. placebo
3. tardive dyskinesia
4. lithium
5. manifest; latent
6. Gestalt
7. response shaping
8. behavioural activation
9. systematic desensitization
10. eclectic; integrative
11. meta-analysis
12. exposure
13. parenting
14. behavioural

MULTIPLE CHOICE

1.	d	10.	b
2.	d	11.	a
3.	a	12.	b
4.	b	13.	c
5.	c	14.	a
6.	c	15.	c
7.	d	16.	c
8.	d	17.	c
9.	a	18.	d

CHAPTER 18

Prevention and Mental Health Promotion in the Community

CHAPTER OUTLINE

LEARNING OBJECTIVES

When you have completed your study of the chapter, you should be able to:

1. Explain how community psychology differs from clinical psychology.

2. Differentiate between primary, secondary, and tertiary prevention.

3. Explain what is meant by mental health promotion, and discuss four key characteristics of mental health promotion identified by Cowen (1996).

4. Describe the three steps that characterize the public health approach to prevention.

5. Discuss the applicability of the public health approach to issues of mental health.

6. Explain how incidence of mental health problems may be related to both risk factors and protective factors.

7. Discuss each of the following pathways toward mental health promotion:

   Attachment

   Competencies

   Social environments

   Empowerment

   Resources to cope with stress

8. Identify and discuss four central mechanisms that, according to Rutter (1987), can help people cope with adversity and develop positive mental health.

9. Differentiate between high-risk and universal approaches to prevention, giving examples of each.

10. Describe the following two prevention programs: the Perry Preschool Project and the Prenatal Early Infancy Project.

11. Discuss the role of the federal government and the provinces in prevention.

12. Discuss two academic-scientific arguments against prevention. How have these arguments been rebutted?

13. Describe five sources of social-political opposition to promotion/prevention.

14. Describe the Better Beginnings, Better Futures project, discussing the ways in which this project is unique.

KEY WORDS

Community psychology _____

_____

Prevention _____

_____

Primary prevention _____

_____

Secondary prevention _____

_____

Tertiary prevention _____

_____

Early intervention _____

_____

Mental health promotion _____

_____

Mental health _____

_____

Public health approach _____

_____

Protective factors _____

_____

Ecological perspective _____

_____

Microsystem _____

_____

Exosystem_____

_____

Macrosystem _____

_____

High-risk approach _____

_____

Universal approach _____

_____

FILL-IN-THE-BLANKS

1. In contrast to the clinical psychology focus on deficits and on reducing maladaptive behaviours, community psychology tends to pay more attention to people's _____ and the promotion of _____.

2. Whereas _____ prevention reduces the duration of a disorder, _____ prevention reduces the incidence of the disorder.

3. The thrust of the _____ approach to prevention is twofold: to reduce environmental stressors while enhancing people's capacities to withstand those stressors.

4. Initial applications of the public health approach to mental health were heavily influenced by the _____ theory of Lindemann and Caplan and were aimed at people just beginning to experience serious mental health problems, striving to nip such problems in the bud.

5. Current thinking is that there are _____ factors that help to offset or buffer risk factors, thus accounting for the fact that some individuals seem stress-resistant.

6. Perceived and actual control over one's life, referred to as _____, is one of several key pathways proposed by Cowen (1994) toward mental health promotion.

7. According to Rutter (1987), one method of helping people cope with adversity is to reduce risk impact. This can be accomplished either by altering the risk or by altering _____ to the risk.

8. There are two major types of prevention programs. The _____ approach is based on the assumption that it is most effective to target individuals who have been exposed to known risk factors. The _____ approach is designed to include all individuals in a particular geographic area or setting.

9. The Perry Preschool Project is a good example of a first-generation _____ prevention program.

10. The Better Beginnings, Better Futures project can be called a _____ prevention program because it was offered to all children in a given age range and their families.

MULTIPLE CHOICE

1. The term _____ was first coined by Canadian psychologist William Line in 1951.

   a. primary prevention
   b. community psychology
   c. mental health promotion
   d. early intervention

2. Whereas _____ has historically focused on the individual or micro level, _____ applies an ecological perspective that stresses the interdependence of the individual, the family, the community, and society.

   a. clinical psychology; community psychology
   b. primary prevention; mental health promotion
   c. primary prevention; secondary prevention
   d. the public health approach; the risk reduction approach

3. Some argue that the term *early intervention* should replace the notion of _____, and that *treatment* or *rehabilitation* should replace _____.

   a. primary prevention; secondary prevention
   b. mental health promotion; prevention
   c. community psychology; clinical psychology
   d. secondary prevention; tertiary prevention

4. According to Albee (1982) the incidence of mental health problems can be viewed as an equation, where incidence =

   a. competencies ÷ resources
   b. prevention ÷ promotion
   c. family circumstances ÷ emotional difficulties
   d. risk factors ÷ protective factors

5. According to the ecological perspective, work settings, schools, religious settings, neighbourhoods, and so on are all examples of the _____.

   a. microsystem
   b. exosystem
   c. macrosystem
   d. social network

6. Which of the following is true concerning the effects of divorce?

   a. Divorce affects young girls more strongly than young boys.
   b. Girls are more likely to feel the consequences of parental divorce later in adolescence.
   c. Parents are more likely to argue in front of girls than boys.
   d. Girls respond to family conflict with disruptive behaviour that is severely punished.

7. According to Rutter (1987), there are four mechanisms that can help people cope with adversity and develop positive mental health. Which of the following is a good example of the mechanism of reducing risk impact?

   a. taking children who need hospitalization to visit the hospital before admission
   b. offering children appropriate tasks and sufficient rewarding experiences of control
   c. teaching youths social skills they can apply in various settings
   d. preventing schooldrop out and ensuring a good education

8. Which of the following is an example of biological secondary prevention?

   a. avoiding alcohol while pregnant
   b. counselling on nutrition provided to pregnant women
   c. administering special diets to children born with PKU
   d. all of the above

9. Some researchers divide high-risk programs into two subtypes: selective and indicated. Indicated programs

   a. select participants on the basis of internal characteristics (e.g., low-birth-weight babies, children experiencing peer rejection, etc.)
   b. select participants on the basis of characteristics external to the participant (e.g., children whose parents have divorced, teenage mothers living on public assistance)
   c. include all individuals in a particular geographical area (e.g., neighbourhood, city, province) or particular setting (e.g., school, housing complex)
   d. are concerned primarily with interrupting unhealthy chain reactions stemming from stressful life events

10. Which of the following is an example of a universal prevention program?

   a. the Perry Preschool Project
   b. the Prenatal Early Infancy Project
   c. the Better Beginnings, Better Futures project
   d. all of the above

ANSWERS

FILL-IN-THE-BLANKS

1. strengths; wellness
2. secondary; primary
3. public health
4. crisis
5. protective
6. empowerment
7. exposure
8. high-risk; universal
9. high-risk
10. universal

MULTIPLE CHOICE

1. b
2. a
3. d
4. d
5. b
6. b
7. a
8. c
9. a
10. c

CHAPTER 19

Mental Disorder and the Law

CHAPTER OUTLINE

LEARNING OBJECTIVES

When you have completed your study of the chapter, you should be able to:

1. Compare the following three primary sources of law in Canada:

    Constitutional law

    Statutory law

    Common law

2. Identify and discuss three criteria that must be met before an individual can be involuntarily hospitalized (also known as civil commitment).

3. Discuss two ways in which release from involuntary hospitalization typically occurs.

4. Explain the role played by a patient's temporary substitute decision maker.

5. Describe two principles outlined in the mental health acts of the 10 provinces and 3 territories that are commonly used in the decisions made by the temporary substitute decision maker.

6. Discuss what research has shown concerning the characteristics of involuntary patients.

7. Discuss what research has shown concerning the outcome of involuntary patients.

8. Contrast the discretionary and nondiscretionary approaches to violent risk assessment.

9. Provide an overview of the HCR-20 approach to risk assessment.

10. Describe what is popularly known as the "insanity defence," as set out in section 16 of the *Criminal Code*.

11. Describe two important English cases from the 1800s—that of James Hadfield and of Daniel M'Naghten—and explain their relevance to the issue of being not criminally responsible on account of mental disorder (NCRMD).

12. Discuss four major amendments made by Bill C-30 in April 1992 to the section of the *Criminal Code* dealing with the disposition of people detained for evaluation of not criminally responsible on account of mental disorder.

13. Explain what is meant by the term *unfit to stand trial* (UST). What is the outcome for someone judged UST?

14. Discuss how fitness evaluations are conducted. Describe the Fitness Interview Test (FIT-R), and explain how it is used.

15. Describe several common misconceptions held by the public concerning the *Criminal Code* provisions regarding mental disorders.

16. Discuss two major ways in which psychologists may be involved with the legal system.

17. Provide examples of some of the activities of forensic psychologists.

18. Distinguish between ethical codes and professional standards.

19. Outline four fundamental ethical principles that comprise the *Canadian Code of Ethics for Psychologists*.

20. Discuss three major themes in the *Specialty Guidelines for Forensic Psychologists*.

21. Discuss the status of psychology in the legal system, contrasting the roles of psychologists with those of physicians.

KEY WORDS

Constitutional law _____

_____

Statutory law _____

_____

Common law _____

_____

Civil code _____

_____

Parens patriae _____

_____

Civil commitment _____

_____

Temporary substitute decision maker _____

_____

Best interests principle _____

_____

Capable wishes principle _____

_____

Community treatment orders _____

_____

Actus reus _____

_____

Mens rea _____

_____

Not criminally responsible on account of mental disorder (NCRMD) _____

_____

M'Naghten standard _____

_____

Unfit to stand trial (UST) _____

_____

Forensic psychology _____

_____

Ethical codes _____

_____

Professional standards _____

_____

Principle of autonomy_____

_____

Principle of nonmaleficence _____

_____

Principle of beneficence _____

_____

Principle of fidelity _____

_____

Principle of justice _____

_____

FILL-IN-THE-BLANKS

1. The inability to perceive accurately or reason correctly about the outside world is referred to as a _____ impairment; the inability to exert adequate controls on one's behaviour is sometimes referred to as a _____ impairment.

2. The law typically _____ *(does/does not)* consider alcohol intoxication to be a mental disorder.

3. The role of mental health professionals in legal proceedings is one of _____.

4. Common law, also referred to as _____ law, is comprised of the decisions of courts, tribunals, and review boards, made on a day-to-day basis.

5. Quebec differs from the rest of Canada in its reliance on a _____ instead of common law.

6. Involuntary hospitalization is also referred to as civil _____.

7. Under provincial mental health acts, psychologists _____ *(are/are not)* legally qualified to determine whether someone meets the criteria for civil commitment.

8. When patients are committed and deemed incapable of making decisions about their treatment, someone must make treatment decisions on their behalf. This person is sometimes referred to as a _____.

9. Temporary substitute decision makers must exercise their judgment according to the principles outlined in the _____.

10. There are two basic approaches to violence risk assessment. The _____ approach is sometimes referred to as clinical, informal, or intuitive, whereas the _____ approach is sometimes referred to as actuarial, mechanistic, or algorithmic.

11. The _____ is a book or manual that describes 20 major risk factors for violence that should be considered in every risk assessment.

12. Under Canadian law, people can be convicted of a criminal offence only when they commit a prohibited act with bad intention. The prohibited act is known as the _____.

13. The _____ has its origins in a well-defined English case and was included almost verbatim in the first *Canadian Criminal Code* in 1894. It has survived virtually intact to the present day and forms the basis for the insanity provisions of the *Canadian Criminal Code*.

14. The _____ is a manual or reference book that presents guidelines concerning how to conduct brief evaluations of competency or fitness to stand trial.

15. _____ are psychologists whose work is intended primarily to assist people in criminal or civil courts or in front of quasi-judicial bodies such as administrative boards and tribunals.

16. To determine what psychologists *should* do in a given situation they turn to _____. Expectations regarding the day-to-day practice or conduct of psychologists are referred to as _____.

MULTIPLE CHOICE

1. Which of the following is *not* part of the definition of mental disorder provided by the law?

   a. internal
   b. unstable
   c. contextual
   d. involuntary

2. In Canada there are three primary sources of law. Which of the following is not one of these?

   a. constitutional law
   b. forensic law
   c. statutory law
   d. common law

3. Which of the following is true concerning statutes?

   a. They cannot be changed or revised unless the constitution is revised.
   b. They tend to be limited to areas of health and mental health.
   c. They must always be consistent with the constitution.
   d. All of the above are true.

4. Mental health law is the only legislative authority in Canada aside from the *Criminal Code* that permits

   a. the detention of people against their will
   b. psychologists to offer their opinions
   c. psychiatrists to act as judges
   d. general practitioners to represent themselves as psychiatrists

5. Which of the following is a criterion, in every province and territory, that must be met for an individual to be involuntarily hospitalized?

   a. The person must be suffering from a mental disorder.
   b. The person must be either unwilling to consent or incapable of consenting to hospitalization on a voluntary basis.
   c. The person must be at risk for causing harm to self or others.
   d. All of the above must be met.

6. Temporary substitute decision makers must exercise their judgment concerning involuntary treatment according to the principles outlined in the provincial mental health acts. Which of the following is not among the principles commonly used?

   a. best interests principle
   b. capable wishes principle
   c. community satisfaction principle
   d actually, all of the above are commonly used

7. In both Crisanti and Love's (2001) study of admissions to the psychiatric unit of the Calgary General Hospital and Grant, Ogloff, and Douglas's (2000) study of patients at Riverview Hospital in British Columbia, those who were involuntarily hospitalized were more likely to be

   a. male
   b. suffering from a personality disorder
   c. adolescent
   d. all of the above

8. Which of the following is *not* true concerning the discretionary approach to violence risk assessment?

   a. It permits mental health professionals to exercise judgment in gathering relevant information and combining the information to make decisions.
   b. It encourages consistency across cases.
   c. It is flexible and easily adapted to new or unusual situations.
   d. It is idiographic, or responsive to the unique characteristics of the case at hand.

9. The 20 risk factors in the HCR-20 fall into three categories. Which of the following is *not* one of these?

   a. historical factors that reflect past or long-term functioning
   b. clinical factors that reflect recent or current functioning
   c. risk management factors that reflect potential adjustment problems based on the patient's plans for the future
   d. burnout factors that reflect the likelihood of the patient withdrawing from programs designed to help him or her control violent impulses

10. Under Canadian law, people can be convicted of a criminal offence only when they commit a prohibited act with bad intention. The bad intention is known as the _____.

    a. *actus reus*
    b. *mens rea*
    c. *spiritus maleficentus*
    d. *intentionus culpabilitus*

11. Which of the following is *not* one of the three elements of the M'Naghten standard?

    a. The accused must have been suffering from a mental disorder.
    b. The accused must not understand the possible consequences of the court proceedings he or she is facing.
    c. The accused must not have known the nature or quality of the act he or she was doing.
    d. The accused must not have known that what he or she was doing was wrong.

12. In the Supreme Court of Canada's judgments in *Cooper v. R* (1980), it was confirmed that a mental disorder includes any disturbance of the mind that is

    a. internal (not the result of situational factors)
    b. intransient (not temporary or ephemeral)
    c. involuntary (not self-induced)
    d. all of the above

13. In Canadian law, people who are unable to participate actively and effectively in their own defence due to a mental disorder are referred to as _____.

    a. not guilty by reason of insanity (NRI)
    b. not criminally responsible on account of mental disorder (NCRMD)
    c. unfit to stand trial (UST)
    d. all of the above

14. Which of the following is *not* one of the three elements of the Canadian Criminal Code definition of *unfit to stand trial*?

    a. unable to know that the act was morally wrong
    b. unable to understand the nature or object of the proceedings
    c. unable to understand the possible consequences of the proceedings
    d. unable to communicate with counsel

15. Which of the following four fundamental ethical principles, set out in the *Canadian Code of Ethics for Psychologists*, is most concerned with the innate worth of every human being?

    a. Respect for the Dignity of Persons
    b. Responsible Caring
    c. Integrity in Relationships
    d. Responsibility to Society

16. Which of the following are major themes apparent in the *Specialty Guidelines for Forensic Psychologists*?

    a. importance of practising within one's area of competence
    b. importance of objectivity and neutrality
    c. need to know and respect the laws governing one's area of practice
    d. all of the above

ANSWERS

FILL-IN-THE-BLANKS

1. cognitive; volitional
2. does not
3. consultants
4. case
5. civil code
6. commitment
7. are not
8. temporary substitute decision maker
9. mental health act
10. discretionary; nondiscretionary
11. HCR-20
12. *actus reus*
13. M'Naghten standard
14. FIT-R
15. forensic psychologists
16. ethical codes; professional standards

MULTIPLE CHOICE

1.	c	9.	d
2.	b	10.	b
3.	c	11.	b
4.	a	12.	d
5.	d	13.	c
6.	c	14.	a
7.	a	15.	a
8.	b	16.	d